MOUNTAINEERS to MAIN STREETS

VIRGINIA

Washington, D.C.
Arlington
Sterling
Rosslyn
Falls Church
Warrenton
Washington
Sperryville
WINCHESTER
Luray
Timberville
Harrisonburg
SHENANDOAH NATIONAL PARK
Charlottesville
Lexington
Covington
Bedford
Lynchburg
Rustburg
Marion
Chatham
Java
DANVILLE
South Boston
RADFORD
FREDERICKSBURG
Caroline County
West Point
Diascund
RICHMOND
Accomac
Onley
Cheriton
Cape Charles
Yorktown
NEWPORT NEWS
PORTSMOUTH
NORFOLK

MOUNTAINEERS to MAIN STREETS

The Old Dominion
as seen through the
Farm Security Administration
Photographs

Brooks Johnson

The Chrysler Museum
Norfolk, Virginia

This catalogue has been supported by a grant from the National Endowment for the Humanities.

Dates of the exhibition: May 3 to June 16, 1985

All photographs, unless noted, are eight-by-ten-inch gelatin-silver prints
from the collection of The Chrysler Museum.

Cover photograph:
Jack Delano
Painting a View of the Shenandoah Valley from Skyline Drive, Near an Entrance to the Appalachian Trail
1940, Dye Transfer Print

The paper in this book meets the guidelines for permanence and durability
of the Committee on Production Guidelines for Book Longevity
of the Council on Library Resources.

Edited by Troy Moss
Designed by Germaine Clair

International Standard Book Number: 0-940744-50-3
Library of Congress Catalog Card Number: 85-71481

The Chrysler Museum, Norfolk, Virginia 23510

Contents

Foreword

The photographers who worked with me in the Farm Security Administration used the camera to interpret and comment on agricultural conditions. Their photographs were widely reproduced in newspapers and magazines and made the public conscious of the need for rural rehabilitation, soil conservation, and corrective farm legislation. The idea content of these photographs combined with fine technique and aesthetic perception resulted in visual images that had a profound effect on the observer.

I became a photographer for the Resettlement Administration in July 1935, immediately after my graduation from Columbia College. During my senior year as a student at Columbia, I worked on a research project for Roy Stryker and Rex Tugwell, who were members of the faculty. I photographed hundreds of lithographs, woodcuts, and etchings from old issues of *Harper's* and *Leslie's Illustrated.* The content and style of these pictures, used as illustrations before photographs could be printed, impressed me. Also, as a founder of the Columbia Camera Club, I met Edward Steichen, Paul Strand, Berenice Abbott, Margaret Bourke-White, and Ralph Steiner, all of whom had a strong influence on my approach to photography.

This was well-defined on my first assignment for the government in the Blue Ridge Mountains of Virginia in 1935. During these early years, I benefited from analyses and critiques by Roy Stryker, Carl Mydans, Walker Evans, and Ben Shahn. There has been little change in my style since the FSA period. My technique has evolved and improved and the subjects of my photographs are different.

My photographic approach for the FSA was direct and straightforward, as it is today. Stryker made me aware of the need to understand the subject and to tell the story in simple, visual terms. I used design and composition to enhance the effect and to make my message clear. My photographs had the prime purpose of being useful and functional. Because I wanted to reach the largest possible audience, I aimed towards expressing the general through the specific.

The most important contribution I made was the Dust Bowl coverage of 1936. These photographs made the entire country aware of the conservation problems in the West and helped create nationwide support for corrective legislation. Combined with Dorothea Lange's migrant photographs, the cause and effect became apparent to all.

My technical problems resulted from long periods on location, the need for high quality, and maintenance of flexibility and mobility. My first camera was the Leica. I also used the Contax, Super Ikonta B, Rolleiflex, and Linhof. I used flashbulbs to illuminate the interiors of rural homes and barns. High aperture lenses on 35mm cameras stopped action and revealed poses, expressions, and scenes that had never been recorded before. The small unobtrusive cameras made photographs possible where complicated equipment would have created antagonism. My five years with the FSA were ones of change, evolution, tension, and sometimes, frustration and despair. They were active, exciting, creative, and stimulating. During these five years, I participated in an educational experience that has influenced my life ever since.

Arthur Rothstein

Preface

During the Depression a small group of government-employed photographers created a remarkable visual document of our culture. The photographs in this catalogue have been selected from among the thousands made by them, now on file at the Library of Congress in Washington, D.C. Although it may seem a tedious endeavor to search through thousands of photographs to locate those which form this work, to me it was a gluttonous visual feast. Each flip of my fingers revealed a new delicacy to gratify my senses. It was clear that this photographic smorgasbord of our American heritage must be experienced by others.

The gourmet selection of 160 photographs reproduced in this catalogue is offered on the occasion of the fiftieth anniversary of the founding of the Resettlement Administration. Unlike the human memory which dims with time, the photograph provides an image as fresh as the moment it was made. Undoubtedly these photographs will bring back many memories to those who lived through this traumatic period in our nation's history. To those born since that time they offer a visual account of an America unknown to the post-World War II generation.

A project of this magnitude is not the work of an individual. There are many people who have given me much help in many different areas. Three of the Farm Security Administration photographers, Arthur Rothstein, Marion Post Wolcott, and Jack Delano, graciously gave me first-person accounts of their activities in Virginia. I hope these narratives have helped give additional worth to the overall work. At the Library of Congress, Beverly Brannan and Leroy Bellamy were helpful in answering my questions and making attributions.

My colleagues at The Chrysler Museum have provided support in many different capacities. David W. Steadman, Museum Director, has enthusiastically supported this project from its inception. He has shown great foresight not only with this project but through his appreciation of photography and the role it has come to play at The Chrysler Museum. My assistant, Karen Twiddy, made the excellent copy prints for the catalogue, and photography intern, Judi Pendry, has also provided assistance with various tasks. Troy Moss, Editor; Irene Roughton, Assistant Registrar; and Joyce Szabo, Curator of American Art have provided invaluable assistance in editing and proofreading the manuscript. The Museum's Chief Librarian, Amy Ciccone, and her staff members, Ann Lobe, Virginia Sites, and Carol O'Reilly have, as usual, secured many inter-library loans and helped with countless other details.

I will also take this opportunity to thank the staff members who worked on the preparation and installation of the exhibition. Catherine Jordan, Registrar, and her staff of Preparators, Willis Potter, Rick Hadley, Bernie Jacobs, and Mike Andrews did a fine job. Also, a usually forgotten thanks to Jim Armbruster and his staff in the mechanical shop. Public Relations were handled by Linda Branche and Molly Dannenmaier. Thanks are also due to Museum staff members, Thomas W. Sokolowski and James F. Sefcik, who were helpful in the early stages of the project but have since gone on to other institutions.

For the purchase of the 160 photographs my thanks to Charles and Judy Hudson and the Horace Goldsmith Foundation. My thanks also to Alice Frank for the loan of books to the exhibition.

I am grateful to the National Endowment for the Humanities for the primary funding to publish this catalogue. My warmest thanks to Robert and Joyce Menschel, who have supported this exhibition and catalogue with the same unfailing encouragement they have given me for many years.

For actual production of the catalogue, my thanks to all of the good people at Teagle and Little printers and especially Susan Young, who supervised production. A special thanks to the designer of this catalogue, Germaine Clair, whose role in this entire project has been much more than can be told here.

My thanks to Dr. Douglass G. Green, Director of the Institute of Humanities; Dr. Peter C. Stewart, Department of History; and Mr. Alf J. Mapp, all of Old Dominion University, who served on my committee where the initial version of this work was submitted as a thesis for a Master of Arts degree in Humanities.

B.J.

A New Image of the Old Dominion

The impression persists that had Rip Van Winkle fallen asleep in early twentieth-century Virginia and awakened twenty, thirty, or even forty years later, the fictitious New Yorker would have found few changes. A respected scholar once described mid twentieth-century Virginia as a "political museum piece" and suggested that the state never accepted the Jacksonian democratic movement of the early nineteenth century.

Indeed there may be some validity in asserting that Virginia changed only slowly, and that the state lagged behind the rest of the country politically and economically. Virginia, it was said, simply refused to join the nation in the new century. Did not concern for the presence of a large minority of blacks make white Virginians want to preserve the status quo? Did not a large farm population tend to promote the conservative values usually associated with rural America? Was not Virginia represented in the United States Senate by two well-known conservatives — Harry Byrd and Carter Glass?

Each of these questions contains a modicum of truth about the Old Dominion, but as the accompanying photographs confirm, a state and its people are far more complicated than any single image can suggest.

Most of the economic traits with which various parts of Virginia are associated were in place in the nineteenth century, the exception being the suburban outreach of the nation's capital. The Eastern Shore had its potatoes, Norfolk its railroads and coal piers, the Southside its tobacco fields, Richmond its cigarette industry, Danville its textiles and tobacco, Roanoke its railroad shops, the Valley its grain and apples, the Southwest its coal mines, Smithfield its hams, and Suffolk its peanuts, all before 1900.

Although this implies that Virginia remained fundamentally unchanged in the twentieth century, the state did experience rather profound changes in the early years of this century. In the thirty years before the Depression, Virginians added to the manufacturing base, diversified agriculture, created more and larger towns, moved into suburbs, built numerous public roads, educated more children for longer school years, fought in a major world war (which drastically changed the state) and generally followed trends, albeit in lesser degrees, observable in other states in the nation.

If Virginia did not do as well as some of the eastern and western states, its laggardness in the 1920s has been exaggerated. The state was unlucky in relying heavily on mining, farming, and cotton textiles: industries that did not prosper in the 1920s. Virginia did add to its material base in the late 1920s, but never attracted the glamour industries of the age — big steel, automobile production, oil, or advertising. The increase in the average size of business firms in the period was due to the elimination of tiny companies rather than the appearance of large organizations. (Exceptions to this trend would be the Ford plant in Norfolk and the DuPont Company in Richmond.)

Rural Virginia trailed many other states in acquiring such conveniences of modern life as electricity and telephones. Cities did better. Richmond was the first city to secure, in the 1880s, electric streetcars. Norfolk acquired dial telephones during World War I, actually well ahead of the rest of the nation. Virginia's cities could be rather advanced in some ways but such receptivity failed to become widespread, especially in rural Virginia.

In the first part of this century the small towns of Virginia were in the ascendancy. In 1920 Virginia contained about eighty communities of one thousand people or more. By 1940 that number had risen to ninety, and most of them were growing. Nearly 90 percent of the towns gained people during this time and indeed had been doing so for the entire century. Curiously, while Virginia's farm population declined, largely because of the migration of blacks, the villages and towns of rural Virginia did not. Such places as Winchester, Fredericksburg, Covington, Marion, and Radford grew steadily before and during the Depression. It would not be going too far to surmise that these growing communities broadened their economies and even benefited from various measures of the New Deal.

Virginia's "conservative" posture is often attributed to the backlash against the participation of former slaves and their offspring in Virginia politics during Reconstruction. This explanation in itself is not adequate. Many states of the Deep South, also with large concentrations of former slaves, accepted some exceedingly radical solutions to various problems. Like other Southern states, Virginia devised means to deprive blacks of the right to vote in the 1890s, and the Constitution of 1902 in fact disenfranchised most blacks. But it also disqualified a great number of white voters, a situation avoided by the Deep South.

Once having accomplished this — and having made their state unique in this regard — Virginia's leaders enthusiastically endorsed nearly every progressive program in vogue throughout the nation. At the same time Virginians were reducing the number of voters, they also established the State Corporation Commission to regulate railroads. The state raised money to upgrade its roads and schools, and municipalities experimented with city manager forms of government. The state even acquired lime plants, and city governments occasionally owned public services. Virginia's brand of conservatism had a decidedly progressive tinge.

World War I and its aftermath brought even more changes. Thousands of people flocked to various defense-related industries in communities like Norfolk, Newport News, Portsmouth, and Hopewell. Problems which naturally accompany such changes compelled all levels of government to react to the crisis by providing numerous services and, in the case of shelter, even federally funded housing. The crisis actually worsened after the Armistice in November 1918 as prices soared and thousands of workers nationwide struck for better wages.

In the midst of all this, a panic struck the market, followed by a steep recession. By the fall of 1920, when Warren Harding was elected president, the worst was over. The economy stabilized. The ensuing decade turned out to be one of comparative prosperity, even though Virginia did not fully share in the economic gains. Most Virginians welcomed the advent of Prohibition, the weakness of labor unions, the deregulation of business by the federal government, and other central features of the period.

This era came to an abrupt end in 1929 with the stock market crash, but Virginians slipped into the Depression only gradually because few individuals in the state had large stock holdings. Although Norfolk contended with a bank failure (whose origins predated the Crash) and Richmond lost the American Bank and Trust Company to receivership in 1932, the state's banks held up well even as "runs" closed down many of these institutions nationally. Eventually the shockwaves of the Crash and the Depression pervaded the state, but even at its worst, the unemployment rate — the principal barometer of the effects of the Depression — of 10 percent remained consistently less than half the national average.

It should not be inferred that Virginians escaped from the Depression unscathed, for thousands did go on relief and countless others lost hours and wages. Virginia contained a great many people who never belonged to the ranks of the industrially employed. For marginal farmers and most blacks in the cities, hard times were all the time.

Some Virginia industries buckled and almost broke. Strikes at the Riverside and Dan River Mills rocked the textile industry. Two of Virginia's railroads were forced into receivership. Early in 1933 the Ford assembly plant closed, throwing several hundred workers into the unemployment lines. In Marion, about 750 furniture workers found themselves out of work when they argued with the Virginia-Lincoln Company over wages and working conditions.

Even a stable enterprise such as Virginia Electric Light and Power lowered prices when major customers like the University of Virginia threatened to build their own power plants. The federal government, usually a reliable employer, temporarily cut back on some work. Claude Swanson, the Secretary of the Navy and a former governor and senator from Virginia, announced that so few veterans were quitting the Navy that the services of the Norfolk Naval Training Station would no longer be needed. Faced with reduced demand, the Naval Shipyard in Portsmouth imposed a forty-hour, five-day workweek. The state and most local governments cut wages 10 to 30 percent.

On the positive side, the state's commercial activity and industrial output, while falling to about 80 percent of its pre-Depression level, did far better than the national decline of 50 percent. And the Federal Reserve Bank in Richmond recorded but a small drop in clearances, with only the Dallas district performing better nationally.

Whether the nation's economy turned the corner on the Depression and started toward recovery in the spring of 1933 because of, or in spite of, President Roosevelt and his New Deal remains a matter of debate. Virginia's newspapers reported harbingers of hope well before Roosevelt's legislation could possibly have taken effect. The president's optimism may have played a role, if only as propaganda. Rumors circulated that millions of the unemployed were returning to work as thousands of factories reopened. A more accurate appraisal was that improvements could be detected.

Although the more exaggerated rumors proved unfounded, conditions gradually improved, especially once Congress approved the National Industrial Recovery Act (NIRA). Under this Act, which created the National Recovery Administration (NRA), businesses were permitted to cooperate with other firms in the same industry to fix prices in return for keeping their plants operating at reasonable capacities with workers paid minimum wages.

At first a popular program, the NRA quickly wore out its welcome. Criticism eventually mounted against it and the Supreme Court later declared the act which created it unconstitutional. But the agency had served its purpose during the emergency.

Despite the comparative strength of the Virginia economy during the crisis, Virginians benefited from many federal programs during the New Deal. Roosevelt's Bank Holiday was well received, for even though the banks in the Old Dominion seemed solvent, they would not have remained so had any appreciable number failed nationally. Other popular programs in Virginia were the Public Works Administration (PWA) and the Civilian Conservation Corps (CCC). The Federal Emergency Relief program turned money over to the states to help the unemployed. The farm inflation measure, eventually known as the Agricultural Adjustment Act, along with the Commodity Credit Corporation, developed a price support system that involved crop restrictions and government storage. The tobacco growers of Southside Virginia, hard hit by low prices, found these programs especially appealing.

It would be hard to imagine two programs more popular in Virginia than the Civilian Conservation Corps and the related parks program. The federal government had cooperated in establishing the Shenandoah National Park as early as 1925. Encouraged by Governor Harry Byrd, the state of Virginia and private interest raised over $2 million for land acquisition (at one time, approximately 360,000 acres). During the Depression plans had to be trimmed to about half the original size, but the idea blended so well with Roosevelt's New Deal that the president strongly backed the construction of the Skyline Drive to allow tourists in motor cars to pass through the park.

Plans for the Shenandoah National Park seemed to whet Virginia's appetite for parklands. The State Commission of Conservation and Development actively encouraged the purchase of land throughout the state. Using a combination of federal, state, and private funds, Virginia established several sites. Twenty-five hundred acres of the Cape Henry Desert became Seashore State Park. Wilson State Park and Battlefield Park near Richmond joined the system. Some fifteen hundred acres were set aside near Clifton Forge for Douthat State Park. Indeed, the commission opened seven parks in 1936 alone.

The Civilian Conservation Corps became closely linked to the preparation of these parks. Newspapers carried numerous references to the young urban recruits who first tasted camp life under the auspices of the Corps. Virginians seemed proud that their state had a large number of these camps, many of which were located in or near the new parks. Nothing quite so well epitomized the spirit of America and Virginia in the 1930s as the efforts of the CCC.

The Skyline Drive may well have been typical of other public works in that it really did not markedly assist recovery efforts until about 1935. Harold Ickes, secretary of the interior, held up funds for it on the grounds that no money was available. The Virginia congressional delegation then demanded a complete disclosure of all PWA spending, and Carter Glass, in threatening to block Roosevelt's massive new recovery effort, met with the president. Roosevelt, who very much favored the road, made sure funds were provided. Other PWA projects included the University of Virginia's Alderman Library, the State Library in Richmond, the Administration Building at the College of William and Mary's extension in Norfolk, a building at Virginia State College, and others. The federal government even picked up much of the tab for Foreman Field at the Norfolk College.

While some projects secured less than 50 percent federal funding, a great many proposals, especially under the Federal Emergency Relief Act, received almost 90 percent. These funds provided invaluable aid to communities with long relief rolls such as Bristol and Norfolk. In conducting these programs the government urged contractors to hire as many unemployed workmen as possible and contract for only minimum purchases of new material. Thus the walls of Foreman Field were composed of mountains of used brick, laboriously cleaned by workers paid a few cents per hour.

Adequate housing was another New Deal concern. Few Virginians took advantage of the special loans that saved many homeowners and lending agencies in the Depression, but the Farm Security and the Resettlement administrations helped create special cooperatives like the Shenandoah Homesteads that took care of mountain families forced off their property by the national park.

During the Depression a great deal of attention was focused on the slums of Virginia's cities. Slums thrived in comparatively new cities like Newport News, only fifty years old, as well as in older cities like Norfolk and Richmond. In Norfolk 12 percent of the population, mostly black, lived on 1 percent of the land, and conditions were equally bad at Bloodfield in Newport News. Norfolk had responded to demands of successful blacks for better roads and sewers in the early 1920s, but conditions remained deplorable in the slums. Leading citizens started to study the question in earnest, but not until after World War II were federal funds tapped to ease the problem. Meanwhile in Newport News, blacks took matters into their own hands by creating Aberdeen Gardens. When the firm that originally financed the project withdrew, the Farm Security Administration stepped in and sponsored it cooperatively with Hampton Institute. Designed by black architects and built by black workmen under the supervision of black foremen, the community of five-to-seven-room homes on one-half acre plots proved to be a great success. So much so that envious whites tried, but failed, to turn the homes over to whites.

Virginia's voters were quite willing to give Roosevelt a chance to launch his New Deal. They might display concern about the defects of the NRA or other specifics, but they were quite willing to support Roosevelt as he cast about for ideas that might work and threw out those that did not. Upon opening the National Park in July of 1936, FDR observed that his government planned to try to "put our idle people to work and end the waste of the land." Most Virginians agreed not only with these goals but with most of Roosevelt's methods, and in the election that fall they refused to side with the voters of Maine and Vermont, the only two states not to vote for FDR in 1936.

By the time of the election, Roosevelt had unveiled what historians call his Second New Deal. Roosevelt and Congress passed measures designed to control big business and collect more taxes from the wealthy. The features of the National Industrial Recovery Act, giving labor the right to bargain collectively, were provided for in the Wagner Act after the demise of the NIRA. The new legislation also included Social Security and an enlarged recovery agency known as the Works Progress Administration (WPA).

The WPA, even though it served as the linchpin of the new recovery program, may have had less direct influence in Virginia than in other states. Its funds did help develop the Azalea Gardens near Norfolk and hired the historically-minded to produce two valuable guides. Both books were ultimately taken over by the Virginia Writers Project. The *Negro in Virginia* remains a remarkable pioneering effort on black history; *Virginia: A Guide to the Old Dominion* could serve as a companion for this collection of photographs. Several painters, playwrights, and other artists also received help from the WPA.

Much has been made of Virginia's adherence to the so-called Byrd Organization during the Depression and after. Actually, Senator Byrd became an opponent to the New Deal only after it was reasonably well advanced. By the time most Virginians recognized Byrd's opposition to the Roosevelt program (principally over monetary deficits) both he and the president were so well entrenched that neither one could be defeated.

The state's voters tended to elect congressmen who supported Roosevelt. Thus six of nine Virginia congressmen voted for the minimum wage in 1938, and an opponent of Social Security and a Byrd man in the Norfolk District for Congress, Colgate Darden, found himself replaced as the Democratic nominee in the 1936 election.

The group of Democrats in Virginia known as the Byrd Organization wielded considerable power and its members opposed several New Deal programs, but often Virginians ignored its advice on crucial questions. Governor George Perry, who entered office in 1934, was viewed as a member of the Byrd Organization, but in his search for federal dollars he sometimes disagreed with Byrd over the New Deal. James Price, who succeeded Perry as governor in 1938, captured the Democratic nomination as a party maverick. He not only opposed the Organization, but was also a staunch New Dealer. It was even rumored that he favored both federal and state deficits. Price was never able to find state approval for a rather progressive counterpart to the New Deal, which included prison reform, but his mere presence in the governor's mansion confirms the moderation of most Virginians during the last stages of the New Deal.

By the fall of 1939 world conditions were rapidly deteriorating. Those vestiges of the Depression that still remained quickly disappeared as Europe went to war. Worry over employment was replaced by a greater fear that the United States might become a direct participant in either the war in Europe or the one in Asia, or both.

By 1940 the state was in the full throes of defense build-up. Huge military outposts such as Fort A.P. Hill, located near Bowling Green in Caroline County, materialized almost overnight. The residents of the affected area were suddenly dispossessed, much as the mountain folk who had to move in the mid-1930s. The Quantico Marine Base throbbed with activity. The Navy base in Norfolk, fairly quiet since the previous world war, quickly acquired more land for its air station and hired thousands of civilians for its varied functions. The Norfolk Naval Shipyard stepped up its maintenance program and added the construction of battleships and aircraft carriers. War-related industries such as the Hercules Powder Plant near Radford hired hundreds of workers.

With the bombing of Pearl Harbor in December 1941, the economy accelerated beyond the wildest dreams of New Dealers. By 1943 the navy yard employed some forty-three thousand workers, a sixfold increase from before the war. The yard actually needed twelve thousand more workers, but they could not be found. Newport News Shipbuilding and Drydock, with many contracts to fill for naval ships, experienced a similar rise in employment and faced the same shortage. With so many military installations, Virginia felt the full effects of the war economy.

The state benefited from expanded employment, but the war brought on another crisis. Thousands of people flocked to the defense jobs only to find cramped living conditions. Bed occupants were sometimes rotated in eight-hour shifts. The tramps prevalent in the Depression were succeeded by hundreds of cars and trailers. The latter often ended up in residential yards because parks for them were not ready. By 1942 there were shortages of nearly everything from gasoline to water and food, schools, and proper sanitation.

During the war the federal government ended the New Deal, an event which took place symbolically when Congress terminated the WPA. But before that happened various agencies helped cushion the dramatic shift to a wartime economy.

Sometimes the move from Dr. New Deal to Dr. Win-the-War was rather subtle. In the matter of housing, for example, the Farm Security Administration, which had been relocating rural people to nearby modern homes, provided the same for rural workers as they and their families moved to larger urban settlements to work in defense jobs.

The New Deal had fostered a great deal of thought about society's needs. Many communities had lengthy wish lists which, despite the massive infusion of federal aid, remained unfulfilled. The coming of the war provided money for such projects if areas hard hit by defense projects could prove a need for it. Similarly, voters seemed more willing to support programs they had earlier rejected, such as the creation of a sewage district involving several cities of Hampton Roads.

In retrospect, the winds of change never stopped blowing in Virginia; they picked up strength with the New Deal and nearly became a hurricane in the Second World War. Despite myths about Virginia's conservatism, the state rode with, not against, the winds. Virginians realistically faced the problems that these winds brought and ultimately benefited from them.

Dr. Peter C. Stewart
Associate Professor of History
Old Dominion University

Introduction

The "Great Depression" and Franklin Delano Roosevelt's New Deal fundamentally altered the structure of American society. During the Depression, photography was used on an unprecedented scale to document an America struggling through the ordeal of massive economic collapse. Under the direction of Roy Emerson Stryker, a quarter of a million negatives were taken and over 100,000 prints were made between 1935-1943. These photographs, housed at the Library of Congress in Washington, D.C., include approximately two thousand made in Virginia. The 160 photographs in this catalogue have been selected from that group.

Although the photographs are usually referred to as having been made by the Farm Security Administration they were actually made under the sponsorship of three United States government agencies. Roy Stryker was director of the Historical Section, a tiny subdivision of the Resettlement Administration. In 1937 the Resettlement Administration became a part of the Department of Agriculture and was renamed the Farm Security Administration.[1] In September 1942, in the midst of the Second World War, Stryker's Historical Section was transferred to the Office of War Information.[2]

Although he was not a photographer, Roy Stryker was the person largely responsible for the richness of this vast resource. He believed that the "photographic" documentation of living history "was an under-used concept." He thought social scientists, historians, and photographers should cooperate in the selection of subjects that would "give the social historian of tomorrow a photographic record that would be concentrated and orderly." Stryker believed that "in photography the historian has . . . a new edge to his tool."[3] The potential of being able to photographically document a culture with everything significant recorded in minute detail was an exciting new prospect. One photograph alone could yield volumes of information to the historian about how people had lived.

Stryker believed that documentary photography should "supply particulars about ourselves" and that these particulars "in their totality reveal a way of life." He imbued his charges with a mission to photographically document America so that the historian of the future could understand what life was like during the Depression. However, Stryker thought that the photographs

are only going to be significant if somebody goes in and takes 15 of them — one of them — 50 of them and does something. He makes an article; he makes an exhibit; . . . he does a magazine.[4]

This catalogue makes 160 photographs, many of which have never been seen outside the Library of Congress, accessible to a larger audience. A criticism of the FSA work is that the same images are seen over and over again. These photographs are often referred to as the "cookie cutters." Among the Virginia work, Arthur Rothstein's Blue Ridge Mountaineers and Marion Post Wolcott's fertile landscapes are the best known. This catalogue attempts to make a more comprehensive presentation of this photographic portrait of Virginia's past. However, it should be noted that not all areas of the state were equally photographed. Thus, the geographic balance of this catalogue is limited by the photographs' locales.

At the Library of Congress, the photographs are stored in file cabinets and are divided into regions of the country: Farwestern, Southwestern, Northwestern, Midwestern, Northeastern, and Southern. In order to identify the photographs made in Virginia it was necessary to review approximately seventeen thousand photographs filed in the Southern section. The filing system makes it easy to find all of the photographs of specific subjects. But unfortunately, it completely destroys the original sequence of the photographs.[5]

Consider Jack Delano's photo-story on the migrant workers and the Norfolk-Cape Charles Ferry. In order to see all of the photographs in this series one has to look under numerous subject headings and even then under several subheadings. Migrant Workers is a subheading under People; Migratory Worker's Camps is a subheading under Home; Migrants' Cars and Ferries are subheadings under Transportation; and Card Games is a subheading under Social Activities. Maintaining a sense of the original series is difficult as one jumps from one file cabinet to another at the Library of Congress. Thus, another contribution of this work is to bring together many photo-stories that have not been seen as such since the present filing system was organized in 1943.[6]

Formed in May 1935, the Resettlement Administration was a component of President Franklin Delano Roosevelt's New Deal. The Resettlement Administration's purpose was to solve the chronic problem of rural poverty in the United States. The head of the Resettlement Administration was Rexford G. Tugwell, a member of FDR's Brain Trust and Roy Stryker's former instructor and colleague in the Economics Department at Columbia College. Although at first it may seem odd for an economics professor, who was not a photographer, to manage a photography project, Tugwell's appointment of Roy Stryker as chief of the Historical Section proved to be sheer genius.

At Columbia, Stryker frequently made use of photographs in the classroom to help explain economics. As Tugwell anticipated problems in making Congressmen and the general public understand the problems of rural poverty, he enlisted Stryker to use photography to explain America to Americans. The concept of using a series of photographs as a method of mass communication was still in its infancy. Television was more than a decade away, and *Life,* the first picture magazine in America, did not appear on the newsstands until November 1936. Tugwell's great foresight was his early recognition of the power of the photographic image to inform and persuade.[7]

The motivation for the photography produced by the Historical Section was not at all the same as for the art programs of the Works Progress Administration. The purpose of the art programs was to give unemployed artists jobs. The purpose of the Historical Section was to provide information about how the New Deal was helping people, specifically farmers. The fact that many of these photographs came to be regarded as art objects is secondary to their original purpose. In 1936, Tugwell wrote "that they may be considered works of art is complimentary, but incidental to our purpose."[8] The art programs employed thousands of artists nationwide while the Historical Section employed in its lifetime less than a score of photographers and then never more than six at any one time.

The Historical Section's photographs were politically inspired and as such must be considered propaganda. Although the government had used photographs pre-viously, these were the first made strictly for partisan purposes. The FDR administration wanted to show the people that agricultural reforms were needed and that the New Deal offered the best hope for change. President Roosevelt was well aware of the value of persuasion: "you can right a lot of wrongs with 'pitiless publicity,'" because social change "is a difficult thing in our civilization unless you have sentiment."[9]

The documentary, or realistic, approach was widespread in the 1930s. Americans believed in the document — it was a fact, something real they could hold on to while the social structure around them crumbled. Social workers, politicians, and the press used statistics to show how bad things were and to embarrass the Hoover administration. The development of a genre of photography known as 'documentary' is closely linked with the Farm Security Administration work. A realistic approach was also evident in other arts: in painting the artist addressed his naturalistic imagery to the masses instead of the moneyed few, the Federal Theater acted out the issues of the day through the "Living Newspapers," and the Federal Writers Project produced hundreds of factual guidebooks and pamphlets on states and major cities. "Art for art's sake" was as worthless as the stocks of Wall Street. With this attitude widespread, it is easy to see why the photographs of the Historical Section, reproduced in newspapers, magazines, and pamphlets, were so believable and thus most persuasive.

The Synthesis of the Section

The Historical Section's work has received wide acclaim not only because of the broad scope of the documentation but because of the consistent quality of the images. Fortunately, this style was shaped early in the life of the agency by Dorothea Lange, Walker Evans, Ben Shahn, and, of course Roy Stryker. The synthesis of philosophy and imagery among these people provided a definite format for the duration of the project.

Roy Stryker was named chief of the Historical Section at a salary of $5,600 per year. His duties were to

> direct the activities of investigators, photographers, economists, sociologists and statisticians engaged in the accumulation and compilation of reports . . . statistics, photographic material, vital statistics, agricultural surveys, maps and sketches necessary to make accurate descriptions of the various . . . phases of the Resettlement Administration, particularly with regard to the historical, sociological and economic aspects of the several programs and their accomplishments.[1]

This bureaucratic job description left Stryker bewildered as to what exactly he was supposed to do. He said, "many think I went down to Washington with a big plan. I didn't. There was no such plan."[2]

Direction for the Historical Section first came from reports, by Paul Taylor and Dorothea Lange, on migrant workers. Prepared for the California Emergency Relief Administration, the reports had been instrumental in securing funds to build camps for migrants. Lange was largely responsible for the presentation which effectively combined photographs, words, and layout to show the plight of the unfortunate. On her own, she had realized the effectiveness of using words and pictures to tell a story. Her style of photography, as exemplified in the migrant reports, became a prototype for the work of the Historical Section. She was hired in August 1935 as the Resettlement Administration's West Coast photographer.[3]

Lange was most concerned with how photography could be used for social change and as historical documents. To her, "art was a by-product . . . a plus something that happens" if your work is "done well enough and intensely enough." She was not at all comfortable with her photographs being considered as art and was embarrassed by the "role of artist."[4]

During the four-year period Dorothea Lange worked for the agency she was terminated twice. This was largely due to budget cutbacks and the distance between her location on the West Coast and the FSA office in Washington. Occasionally Lange worked on a part-time basis. During the summer of 1938 she was paid three dollars for each negative selected to become a part of the file. Her Richmond photograph was made at this time and might help to explain why there is only one image taken in the Virginia capital. As the FSA was primarily concerned with rural problems, Richmond, at the time the largest city in Virginia, would have been generally avoided. Perhaps, in his constant effort to provide a comprehensive portrait of America, Stryker purchased Lange's Richmond photograph because he knew there were no others of that city.

Lange's other Virginia photographs depict an idealized rural America. Her photograph of *Men Cradling Wheat* is a lyric image that markedly resembles a nineteenth-century French landscape painting. Lange's photograph of *A Wheat Field* offers a tranquil view of the Virginia countryside. This type of photograph seems to have been almost obligatory in Virginia, as both Rothstein and Wolcott made similar views of the rolling hillsides showing the effects of man's cultivation on the terrain. Although Lange and Evans made few photographs in Virginia their influence over those who did work in the state was considerable.

Dorothea Lange's — and Stryker's — approach to photography was in sharp contrast to Walker Evans's, who also made significant contributions to the Historical Section's style. Evans was hired in October 1935 at a higher salary than the other photographers. He was able to demand more because he had somewhat of a reputation; among other achievements he had made photographs for Carleton Beals's book, *The Crime of Cuba*, published in 1933.

Evans would later admit that he took the job only as a way to travel around the country and make photographs at the government's expense. Evans detested the government's bureaucracy, and he proved to be a constant problem for Stryker. In order to achieve maximum quality in his photographs, Evans used a cumbersome eight-by-ten inch camera. This caused him to work slowly, and from the bureaucrats' standpoint, unproductively. He would often disappear for weeks and would occasionally refuse to make routine photographs. Whereas his output was much lower than the other photographers, the quality of his work was much higher.[5]

In the 1920s Evans, who was living in New York, became "nauseated" with America and its big business attitude. He moved to Paris for two years, took classes at the Sorbonne, and became involved with the artistic temperament of the time. Most importantly, he was exposed to the photographs of Eugène Atget and Nadar. These experiences influenced Evans and served as the guiding spirit for his own work.

Walker Evans's experience as an expatriate and member of the New York cognoscenti gave him direction in his photography. Stryker recognized Evans's sophistication and was shrewd enough to learn what he could from him. But because of fundamental differences in their philosophies toward photography, the relationship between them was doomed from the beginning. In opposition to Stryker's beliefs, Walker Evans was not interested in making photographs for historical or sociological purposes. Evans's concern was to make photographs that would be considered works of art. Stryker saw the camera as a tool that could make the most effective kind of document. For Evans, the camera was a machine through which the artist's mind worked. Evans believed that "with the camera, it's all or nothing. You either get what you're after at once, or what you do has to be worthless." Evans's quest for perfection set an example that influenced every other photographer who worked for the FSA, with the possible exception of Dorothea Lange.[6]

In 1938, Evans had an exhibition at the Museum of Modern Art in New York City. The exhibition was accompanied by the publication of *American Photographs*. The images were reproduced one to a page with the facing page left blank. The photographs were divided into two groups, with captions at the end of the sections. The first part, according to Lincoln Kirstein's essay published in the book, could be labeled "People by Photography" and reveals the "physiognomy of a nation." The second part is concerned with the "indigenous American expression" in "whatever form it has taken."[7] Although in the book these photographs are viewed individually, when considered collectively they give a sense of the American culture in the 1930s. These photographs do for Depression-era America what Eugène Atget's photographs did for turn-of-the-century Paris. They describe a place and time but because of the purity and beauty of the images they are timeless.

There are only two Walker Evans photographs made in Virginia on file at the Library of Congress. Apparently Evans liked them enough to reproduce both in two important publications of his work. They appeared in the second part of *American Photographs* and in *A Vision Shared* by Hank O'Neal, a book published in reaction to the "cookie cutter" mentality of repeatedly using the same photographs. O'Neal had each of the living FSA photographers select the images they wanted reproduced in the book. Evans, who died before the book

was published but after his work on it was completed, selected his two Fredericksburg photographs for inclusion. However, there was one significant change in the presentation of the photographs. In *American Photographs* the images were slightly smaller than actual size and were cropped. The photographs show six simple frame houses from two angles, front and side. The frontal view was cropped to a rectangle even more pronounced than a 35mm format. The two wires in the upper right hand corner were completely missing from the composition. The side view was cropped into a square format with the entire trunk of the tree on the left missing. While purists may shudder to think of Evans cropping his photographs so drastically, his views on the subject are surprising. In 1971 he said, "I'll do anything to get one photograph. That's another matter I would have to quarrel with a man like [Alfred] Stieglitz [who]. . . . wouldn't cut a quarter of an inch off a frame. I would cut any number of inches off my frames in order to get a better picture."[8] Apparently in the thirty-eight-year span between publication of the two books he decided that he preferred his original version better. *A Vision Shared* reproduced the photographs full frame, larger than their original eight-by-ten inch size, and facing each other.

Ben Shahn also deserves mention as being instrumental in clarifying the direction of the Historical Section. Shahn, who was employed by the Special Skills Division of the Resettlement Administration, frequently used a Leica 35mm camera as a way to make quick studies for his paintings.

Shahn was not afraid of the word propaganda. He thought that propaganda could be used effectively to instruct others. He helped Stryker understand how photographs could move people. Shahn explained that a photograph of eroded soil would not affect anyone, but a photograph of a child who is starving because the soil is eroded has emotional impact.[9]

Dorothea Lange, Walker Evans, and Ben Shahn were sensitive artists who in their own ways used the camera as a tool. They gave Stryker and the Historical Section the photographic direction that was vitally needed. But it was Stryker who guided and sustained the project throughout its eight-year life.

Dorothea Lange
Three Rooms for Rent, Twelve Dollars per Month
Richmond, August 1938

Dorothea Lange
Men Cradling Wheat
Near Sperryville, June 1936

Dorothea Lange
Wheat Field in Rural Virginia
July 1936

Walker Evans
Frame Houses
Fredericksburg, March 1936

Walker Evans
Frame Houses
Fredericksburg, March 1936

A New Deal in Housing

I want to start tonight with the words which were used in a letter to me a short time ago ... "when you found me, I was crawlin ... now I'm walkin." A simple statement, but there was a lot behind it. It came from the lips of Stanley Moore of Virginia, one of the 420,000 farm families — the 2 million men, women, and children — the Resettlement Administration has helped. It was his own way of saying what the word "rehabilitation" meant to him. When our rural supervisor found him, trying to support his wife, two children, and three grandchildren on 18 acres of undernourished land, he was in reality "crawlin' ... bogged down in debt, poverty and distress. The depression had robbed him of his capital; he couldn't obtain the necessary fertilizer for his land, nor the livestock which could supply either food or animal power. He had, in fact, little more than the shirt on his back, plus a determination that somehow he would get off the relief rolls and cease being a burden to his friends and government.

Stanley Moore needed two things. He needed some money with which to get underway again; and he needed to be shown how he could manage his small farm so as to get the maximum out of it. When he applied to the Resettlement Administration, we inquired about him among his neighbors. They all said that if any man deserved help, it was Stanley Moore, not only because he *needed* help, but because he was honest, reliable, and willing to work. We decided to make him a loan. With it he bought some fertilizer, seed and livestock. The county supervisor helped him work out a plan of management for his 18 acres that would give him, first, a good food supply; second, food for his animals; and third, a cash income. He made the most of this opportunity and now he is no longer crawlin, 'he is walkin' ... out of the relief ditch up the road to self-respect and independence. He has already made the first payment on his government loan.

That, in simple human terms, is what the rehabilitation program of the Resettlement Administration is. It is a program designed to give the distressed farmer a new opportunity to earn an honest and decent living. Not all of our people work out as well as Stanley Moore did. But enough do to make it worthwhile.[1]

So began Rexford Tugwell's address over the Columbia Broadcasting System on February 6, 1936. The Resettlement (and later the Farm Security) Administration managed various programs to help farmers. They provided low-cost loans and actually built new housing for the poor. Within the RA and FSA the Division of Subsistence Homesteads managed the construction of housing. It was the only agency with the exclusive purpose of building whole communities, and it proved to be one of the most problematic of the New Deal programs.[2]

The novel concept of building planned communities was enthusiastically supported by President and Mrs. Roosevelt. Arthurdale, a Subsistence Homestead in West Virginia, became the pet project of Mrs. Roosevelt. She assumed a semiofficial position and helped in its planning and administration, sometimes to the chagrin of those officials responsible for the project.[3] The philosophy behind Subsistence Homesteads was that families could raise nearly all of their food while working nearby in part-time industrial employment. The homesteads varied from two to five acres per family and were grouped in communities of twenty-five to 125 units.[4] Approximately one hundred of these communities were constructed during the New Deal. These communities caused controversies because they were thought to be communist in nature. To combat the attacks of those who did not agree with the New Deal, the Resettlement Administration used the photography project as a propaganda tool. The photographs demonstrated how the New Deal programs were helping Americans. Photographing the government housing projects was a frequent assignment given to the photographers. Although this was hardly exciting from the photographer's standpoint it was a chore necessary to keep the Information Division functioning.

Virginia had two Subsistence Homestead projects that were the subject of photography by the Resettlement Administration. Shenandoah Homesteads was built to house people who were dispossessed by the creation of the Shenandoah National Park in the Blue Ridge Mountains. Newport News Homesteads was built to house blacks who lived in the slums of that area.

The establishment of the Shenandoah National Park was authorized by the United States Congress in May 1925.[5] The park, located in the Blue Ridge Mountains between Front Royal and Waynesboro, Virginia, began as a conservation effort. But the project fit in perfectly with other objectives of the Roosevelt Administration. The project took ten years to complete as two million dollars had to be raised to purchase the 3,870 separate tracts that constituted the parkland. The Virginia State Legislature provided one million dollars. The Shenandoah National Park Association was established to raise the additional one million. The association did this through its "Buy an Acre" campaign. For a six dollar donation an individual could purchase one acre of parkland and receive a certificate to that effect. The parkland encompassed 275 square miles in 1935 when its title was conveyed from the State of Virginia to the United States Government. The construction of the park's trails, picnic areas, campgrounds, and landscaping was done primarily by the Civilian Conservation Corps. The Park was officially dedicated on July 3, 1936. The ceremony was radio-broadcast throughout the country with President Roosevelt and Secretary of the Interior Ickes present.[6]

There were 480 to 500 families living in the park area who had to be relocated. These people, the descendants of pre-American Revolution pioneers, still used only hand tools and horse-drawn carts. Living on submarginal farms of approximately five acres, they had not really been affected by the Depression. They had been desperately poor ever since the Civil War. Of 465 families living in the park area in 1934, over half had annual incomes of less than one hundred dollars per year. Three hundred and eight of those families reported incomes earned as laborers, forty-nine as farmers, thirty reported no income and seventeen gave moonshine production as their source of income.[7] The isolation imposed by the rugged mountain terrain and the attendant poor transportation caused these people to live in a state relatively unchanged for generations. Because of their limited contact with people outside the mountains, intermarriages were frequent and many still spoke with Elizabethan dialects.[8]

In spite of the need for better living conditions, many of the mountain people did not want to be resettled. They were independent, self-sufficient people who did not want the government interfering in their lives. One letter of protest, written by Will Bailey and thirty others to the Resettlement Administration, reads, "Don't beleave in mooven these famileys out of there homes in the Park era . . . We all beleave in letting thes mountain people stay wher tha are at as long as tha are not in the way."[9]

The Shenandoah Homesteads plan became even more of a problem for the government when Virginia Senator Harry F. Byrd took a dislike to the work of the Resettlement Administration. Byrd likened the resettlement to Soviet communism and constantly harped on the inefficiency within the agency. He described the Resettlement Administration as "a permanent monument to a waste and extravagance such as has never before been known in a civilized country."[10] When the first houses in Shenandoah Homesteads cost eight thousand dollars Byrd retorted that they could have been built by a private contractor for nine hundred. (The high cost was due to expensive wells and installation of modern conveniences.) In the final tally, the average cost per unit was $6,357, including the cost for the land, road building, and management.[11]

Newport News Homesteads, also known as Aberdeen Gardens, was the first resettlement community built specifically for blacks. The Division of Subsistence Homesteads adopted the position early on that blacks should benefit along with whites in the homesteads program. At a March 1935 conference within the division it was decided that 10 percent of the homesteaders should be black.[12]

Aberdeen Gardens was sponsored by Hampton Institute. The project, located on Aberdeen Road, was to be "for the resettlement of Negro shipyard workers, longshoremen, and other low-income Negro families from the slum areas of Newport News, Hampton, and neighboring towns."[13] It was built entirely by black WPA workers at a cost of 1.4 million dollars. When the 158-unit Project was completed, local residents tried to have it converted to a white residence. This was prevented by the Resettlement Administration's director, Will Alexander.[14]

Aberdeen Gardens considerably improved the standard of living for its black residents. The photographs made of the black communities of Newport News and the subsequent photographs of the homesteads were ample proof of the New Deal's accomplishments.

The Dispossessed of the Blue Ridge

The first photographer Stryker hired to work for the Resettlement Administration was Arthur Rothstein. Born in New York City, Rothstein had rarely left Manhattan Island when he went to Washington D.C. He thought the job would give him a good opportunity to see other parts of the United States. Although he had majored in chemistry at Columbia College, Rothstein had an active interest in photography. He had been involved with it since high school and, in his senior year at Columbia, copied pictures for a book Roy Stryker was planning. It was to be a photographic source book on American agriculture, but was never completed. Rothstein began work for the Resettlement Administration in July 1935. He established the agency's darkroom facilities, ordered the necessary photographic equipment, and started hiring darkroom technicians.[1]

Arthur Rothstein's first shooting assignment came in October 1935. He was sent to the Blue Ridge Mountains to photograph people who were being relocated to make way for the Shenandoah National Park. Of this trip, Rothstein says that

> it was a great adventure to me ... I looked at everything with fresh eyes. I was not at all jaded by seeing something over and over again. To me all these things were exciting, seeing a new way of life and I responded to it by taking photographs of what seemed interesting to me, a city boy, coming into a rural area.[2]

Although he spoke with a different accent, Rothstein ingratiated himself into the mountain community by living in a mountain cabin, "being friendly and direct, honest and without pretense," and by giving candy to the children and cigarettes to the adults. At first, he did not attempt to take any photographs, choosing instead to develop a rapport while merely carrying the camera around his neck. This approach was aided by his choice of a 35mm Leica camera. Its miniature format was still somewhat unconventional at that time, but the Leica's inconspicuous size, quietness, and ease of operation made it a perfect choice. Rothstein began taking pictures with the Leica but after some time used his large-format camera in order to make more detailed pictures.[3] A good example of his large-format camera work (3¼ x 4¼-inch negative size) can be found in the environmental portrait of Postmaster Brown of Old Rag. Rothstein offers an analysis of the photograph:

> you see this man in his environment and by studying the picture a little bit you get to learn a great deal about the kind of complex personality that he is. He's not just an ordinary hillbilly postmaster — he's a man who reads books as you can see by the fact that there are several books on the table as well as the one he has in his hand. He also is a religious man — you can see that by the sign "As Christ is the head of the house, the unseen guest at every meal, the silent listener to every conversation" and also he obviously

has either traveled to Europe or he is familiar with places in Europe because he has a large picture of the Colosseum of Rome above the table on the wall. But then there is a frivolous side to his nature which is indicated by the coy picture of a half clad beautiful young lady hanging behind him on the wall with a party wreath thrown over it. He obviously is man who knows how to have fun. And this man who seems to be a small town postmaster is really a complex person and you learn all of that from studying this picture.[4]

Because many of Rothstein's photographs from this series depict people in very primitive states, the Postmaster Brown photograph provides a more balanced view of the mountain folk. Although educational facilities were generally poor, some people could read and write and were aware of the world outside their mountain communities. Postmaster Brown's community of Old Rag built a public school in 1871, and by the 1920s had a school term of nine months. Conversely, as of 1930, Corbin Hollow (where Rothstein made his quaint school house photograph) had no more than nine months total schooling in its entire history.[5]

Postmaster Brown and *Mountain Cabin Interior* were both made possible because of a new product, the flashbulb. The FSA photographers were among the first to make regular use of the flashbulb, which had become commercially available in the 1930s. The flashbulbs were large — 150 watt size — and as Arthur Rothstein remembers, "they frequently went off in your hand, leaving a burn."[6]

Arthur Rothstein freely admits that Ben Shahn and Walker Evans were major influences on his early development as a photographer.[7] His Blue Ridge Mountain work is strongly reminiscent of the photographs made by Walker Evans while living among three families of Alabama sharecroppers. This work by Evans was published in the widely acclaimed book written by James Agee, *Let Us Now Praise Famous Men*. Some of the most striking similarities can be seen in the interior view, *Mountain Cabin Interior*, and the portraits, *Fennel Corbin, Mrs. Bailey Nicholson,* and *The Miller*. These images show the same stylistic aspects of Walker Evans's photographs — a studied, factual observation rendered in intricate detail. The surprising point, though, is that Rothstein's photographs were made nine months before Evans began his celebrated Alabama work (although Evans had been working in this manner for some time before October 1935). The direct similarities between the photographs mentioned is compelling evidence that Rothstein was not only a quick study but was already helping to shape the Resettlement Administration's style.

Arthur Rothstein photographed the primitive way of life endured by the people of the Blue Ridge Mountains. Alone, the photographs had little propaganda value other than to show the mountaineer's poverty, but they had great value when juxtaposed with photographs of people living in the new government housing projects. Marion Post Wolcott and Paul Carter photographed the same mountain people living in the Resettlement Administration housing project near Luray, Ida Valley Farms.[8] Although these photographs are less particularized than Rothstein's, the improved quality of life is readily apparent.

Before joining the FSA, Marion Post Wolcott was working as a feature and fashion photographer for the Philadelphia *Evening Bulletin*. When she was hired, at the end of 1938, the FSA was undergoing a conscious shift in its philosophy towards subject matter. Until that time, most of the FSA photographs showed people in distressed circumstances. Because not everyone was poor, weak, old, or living in an impoverished condition, Stryker saw the need to photograph a more favorable vision of America. Wolcott's photographs romanticized their subjects, providing a view of the more positive side of rural America. Wolcott was much like Rothstein in that she had come from an urban background and enjoyed that same freshness of vision of the rural landscape.[9]

Authur Rothstein's photographs document the mountaineer's independent but primitive way of life before it vanished. Labor-saving devices, educational facilities, medical care, and job opportunities became available to the formerly destitute people. Living in planned communities caused a marked change in the basic lifestyle of the mountaineers, but in this case, it was a change for the better.[10]

Arthur Rothstein
View at Sunset, Stony Man Mountain
Shenandoah National Park, October 1935

Arthur Rothstein
Main Street, Nethers
Shenandoah National Park, October 1935

overleaf:
Arthur Rothstein
A Fertile Plateau in the Blue Ridge Mountains
Shenandoah National Park, October 1935

22

Arthur Rothstein
The Home of Fannie Corbin, Corbin Hollow
Shenandoah National Park Area, October 1935

Arthur Rothstein
Fennel Corbin, Who Is Resettled on New Land
Corbin Hollow, Shenandoah National Park, October 1935

Arthur Rothstein
Mrs. Bailey Nicholson, Nicholson Hollow
Shenandoah National Park Area, October 1935

Arthur Rothstein
The Miller, Nethers
Shenandoah National Park, October 1935

Arthur Rothstein
Dicee Corbin's Cabin, Corbin Hollow
Shenandoah National Park, October 1935

Arthur Rothstein
A Mountaineer's Cabin, Corbin Hollow
Shenandoah National Park, October 1935

Arthur Rothstein
Home of a Family Who Are Being Moved to the Homesteads
Old Rag, Shenandoah National Park, October 1935

Arthur Rothstein
The Son of a Squatter Seated in a Doorway, Corbin Hollow
Shenandoah National Park, October 1935

Arthur Rothstein
The School House, Corbin Hollow
Shenandoah National Park, October 1935

Arthur Rothstein
The Church, Nicholson Hollow
Shenandoah National Park, October 1935

Arthur Rothstein
Home of Postmaster Brown, Old Rag
Shenandoah National Park Area, October 1935

Arthur Rothstein
Inhabitants in Front of the Post Office, Nethers
Shenandoah National Park, October 1935

Arthur Rothstein
Post Office, Nethers
Shenandoah National Park, October 1935

Arthur Rothstein
Spreading Apples to Dry on a Roof, Nicholson Hollow
Shenandoah National Park, October 1935

Arthur Rothstein
Roadside Stand
Shenandoah National Park, October 1935

Arthur Rothstein
Russ Nicholson Peeling Apples, Nicholson Hollow
Shenandoah National Park, October 1935

Marion Post Wolcott
Planting Corn
Shenandoah Valley, May 1941

Paul Carter
Looking East from Pasture Hill, Ida Valley Farms
Luray, March 1936

Marion Post Wolcott
Some of the Homes, Ida Valley Farms
Luray, May 1941

Marion Post Wolcott
House and Barn, Ida Valley Farms
Luray, May 1941

Marion Post Wolcott
Working in the Field, Ida Valley Farms
Luray, May 1941

Aberdeen Gardens and Newport News

Paul Carter began working as a photographer for the Resettlement Administration in late 1935. His brother, John Franklin Carter, was the head of the Information Division of which the Historical Section formed a part. Although he could make satisfactory pictures, it seems that Carter lacked an "eye," a sense of what constitutes a good photograph. Because of this, he worked at the Resettlement Administration for only about a year. It was near the end of his tenure, September 1936, that he went to Newport News.[1]

Carter's photographs focus primarily on the black community of Newport News. They include such scenes as a blacksmith shop or a market, but most appear to be simply random views made in the black section of town. One of his photographs depicts two types of houses in Newport News Homesteads.

Little more than a year after Carter's visit, in October 1937, as Aberdeen Gardens was nearing completion, Arthur Rothstein also went to Newport News. He was accompanied by John Vachon, who had been hired in the summer of 1936 as an assistant messenger at a salary of $1,080 per year.[2] Vachon, who had an English degree from Catholic University, carried few messages; his real job was to copy the captions onto the backs of photographs and stamp them with the appropriate photographer's name. After doing this simple task for several weeks, he took the time to study a Walker Evans photograph of a fruit stand. It stimulated his interest enough to look at other photographs coming into the agency's office. On a daily diet of photographs by Evans, Lange, Shahn, and Rothstein, Vachon assimilated the varied styles of these artists. He learned what the FSA photographers looked for in their wide-ranging travels throughout America.[3]

Soon Vachon wanted to photograph scenes that he felt needed to be in the file. Ben Shahn showed him how to use a 35mm Leica, but Walker Evans believed Vachon should first learn how to photograph with an eight-by-ten-inch view camera. So he received photographic instruction from both of these exceptional, though different, artists. This, combined with his new job of organizing the thousands of photographs into a coherent system, gave Vachon a unique perspective on the entire FSA photography project. He began his own photographic explorations in the Washington environs on the weekends.[4]

Vachon's first overnight trip for the FSA was the visit to Newport News in the company of Arthur Rothstein. This trip proved to be a memorable experience for both men. Arthur Rothstein recalls that they left Washington together in his Model A Ford. Rothstein was to be a "kind of technical advisor" to Vachon, although "in many ways he resented my telling him anything about how to take a picture, since he had very definite ideas about what he wanted to do."[5] Rothstein's observation of the younger man's resentment is upheld by Vachon's account of this same trip:

> Rothstein and I spent two days photographing the project [Aberdeen Gardens] and then drove back to Washington by way of the Skyline Drive. Late in the afternoon we found a promontory off a side road with a view of a deserted log house and a splendid vista of mountains fading away in the west in varigated hues of deep and misty blue.... I set up the 8 by 10 inch view camera, went under the black cloth, and spent several minutes focusing, adjusting the rising front, composing in the ground glass, waiting for the sun to just glint the edge of a cloud. Then I emerged, cocked the shutter, inserted a tremendous piece of emulsified film enclosed in a wooden film holder, withdrew the slide, and, holding my breath, I squeezed the cable release. Rothstein thereupon pulled out his Leica and snapped three variations of my scene "Just to cover you in case ... " he said. Of course, I forgave him. About sixteen years later.[6]

The photographs made by Rothstein and Vachon on this trip are of a just-completed Aberdeen Gardens. The homesteaders are pictured moving into their new brick homes. The importance the homesteaders placed on this move can be seen in Rothstein's photograph of the couple inspecting the furnace and stove. They are dressed in their "Sunday best": he in a suit and tie and she with a cloak trimmed in fur and a dangling necklace.

While in Newport News, Vachon made a series of photographs as random as those made a year earlier by Carter. Vachon's photographs, however, show more sensitivity to the medium than do Carter's. His *Street Scene* uses a shadow, extending tentacle-like across the photograph, as a compositional device. The *American Institute of Music* captures the delicate reflections of trees in the windows. Both of these images have the signs and architectural details required by the documentary photographer, but these photographs also reveal Vachon's awareness of how the medium can be used to make pleasing images.

At first Vachon's *Street Corner* appears to be merely a random snapshot. But because of the juxtaposition of the elements — the man, mail box, trash can, background storefronts, the two strong vertical elements created by poles in the foreground, and of course, the signs — a more sophisticated vision is revealed. Normally these everyday sights would be ignored, but Vachon forces the viewer to see the chaotic environment of the man and, by extension, the people of the time.

Paul Carter
A Market in the Negro Section
Newport News, September 1936

Paul Carter
View of Life in the Negro Section
Newport News, September 1936

Paul Carter
A Blacksmith Shop in the Negro Section,
the Only One in the City
Newport News, September 1936

Paul Carter
View of Life in the Negro Section
Newport News, September 1936

Paul Carter
Fishing Boats in the Harbor
Newport News, September 1936

Paul Carter
Front View of Type A and B Houses
Newport News Homesteads, September 1936

John Vachon
Some of the Completed Houses
Newport News Homesteads, October 1937

Arthur Rothstein
Moving into One of the New Houses
Newport News Homesteads, November 1937

Arthur Rothstein
Inspecting the Furnace and Stove in One of the Houses
Newport News Homesteads, December 1937

Arthur Rothstein
People Moving into Their New Home
Newport News Homesteads, November 1937

John Vachon
American Institute of Music; A Window Sign
Newport News, November 1937

John Vachon
A Street Scene
Newport News, November 1937

John Vachon
Curb Service
Newport News, November 1937

John Vachon
A Street Corner
Newport News, November 1937

The Small Town Aesthetic

Before John Vachon made his trip to Newport News in 1937 he refined his photographic skills close to home. He wrote that

> for the rest of that summer I carried a heavy case and tripod around Washington photographing architectural oddities after the manner of Walker Evans. I remained a weekend photographer, but many of my photographs were accorded the consummate honor: they were added to the File.[1]

His photographs made in Falls Church and Rosslyn were most certainly made on those weekend excursions. The subjects depicted are architecturally unusual. The photographs, unmistakably in the Evans style, were made with a four-by-five inch large-format camera. The file that Vachon refers to was, of course, the repository for all of the agency's photographs. Because he had been promoted to file clerk, which meant that he organized and filed the photographs coming into the agency, Vachon knew "this vast collection of photographs better than anyone else in the world"[2] But the file was not growing in a haphazard fashion. Through periodic review of the file and the use of numerous shooting scripts, specific subjects were sought out by the FSA photographers.

The impetus for the scripts came from an encounter between Roy Stryker and Robert Lynd, who, with his wife Helen, had published *Middletown: A Study in American Culture.*[3] Lynd and Stryker discussed the potential of using photography as a tool for social documentation. The possibility of undertaking a photographic study of American small-town life was a fascinating concept for the two men. This led Stryker to devise an outline, or script, to direct his photographers to the significant aspects of small-town life. This shooting script became a standard part of the FSA photographer's equipment.[4]

Although there was no official justification for the small-town documentation, it became a compelling objective in the Historical Section. The following excerpt from a preface to a small-town outline gives some idea of how this was accomplished:

> Because of the importance of the Small Town in American rural life, every Farm Security Administration photographer carries a permanent small-town shooting-script. Whether he goes on assignment to cover projects in Ohio or migrants in Texas, that shooting script is in his pocket, and, often read, to a large extent in his head. As he drives along, through hundreds of towns, he cannot help but run into items on the script. He stops the old bus, shoots, and goes on. Only occasionally does he remain overnight when some special event intrigues him. For, to him, the Small Town is a perennial rather than a special assignment. That shooting script in his pocket is an environment for his curiosity and ingenuity as long as he remains on staff.[5]

The script covered every conceivable activity that might take place in a small town. Some examples of subjects in the script are "men loafing and talking," "Saturday afternoon," "window shopping," "cars and trucks — parked and in transit," "theaters," "restaurants and cafes, shots of windows showing menus and specials," "people — going to church, coming out of church," "the people of the town at their work," "lodges," "recreation."

An essential part of the small-town script was "Main Street." The countenance of Main Street gave each town its individuality, and at the same time linked it with all other small towns in America. This singular expression of a town's identity was photographed routinely. Geography dictated the appearance of a Main Street. Such factors as hills, flat terrain, or nearby bodies of water determined the physical character of the street, but the common denominator throughout America was that Main Street was the place around which transportation arteries formed, commerce thrived, and where human interaction took place. These traits epitomized the character of a small town better that any other single location.[6]

The creation of a pictorial record of rural American culture became a paramount concern for the Historical Section. Undoubtedly, this was the first time that such an ambitious project had been attempted. However, these photographs were not of the news variety; instead, they were of everyday, commonplace scenes. Stryker thought it was significant that in the FSA file there was "only one picture of Franklin Delano Roosevelt, the most newsworthy man of the era." He explained that a news picture could be considered as a noun or a verb while an FSA picture was more akin to an adjective or adverb. The news picture showed action while the FSA picture showed what was behind the action.[7] It is a mistaken notion that newspapers document a culture on a daily basis. In journalism it is the unusual or tragic that is worthy of mention. Newspapers do not publicize the threads of everyday life which together make up the fabric of a culture. Ordinary events are not news.

The small-town photographs are among the most memorable of the FSA's work. To help publicize the photographs, the Historical Section approached Sherwood Anderson with the idea of writing a book based on the FSA's small-town photographs. At the time, Anderson (the author of short stories and novels including *Winesburg, Ohio,* and *Dark Laughter*) was living outside of Marion, Virginia. Anderson first went to Marion, a small town of 4,000 population, in 1925 because of health problems. He liked the small-town atmosphere there and purchased the two local newspapers which he operated with an "intensely local" viewpoint.[8] Edwin Rosskam, who had been hired two years earlier as an editor for the Historical Section, coordinated production of the book. The result of the collaboration between Anderson and the FSA, published in 1940, was *Home Town.*

Many of the photographs by Vachon and Rothstein included in this section would have little value for the bureaucrat, but as visual records of rural America in the late 1930s, they are priceless. Vachon's photographs, *An Ice House, Rosslyn* and *A General Store, Diascund* show the quaintness that one would expect from these establishments. The bewildering array of signs present in these images was intentionally included by the FSA photographers because they believed it would help the historian of the future understand the time in which the image was made. Vachon carried this search to the extreme in his Rosslyn photograph simply titled *Signs.* The signs inform us about the popular culture (or is it consumption?) of the thirties. We see the various types of cigarettes, chewing tobacco, soft drinks, fertilizers, and animal foods with which people living at the time would have been familiar. Vachon's Falls Church photograph, with a water tower looming behind a church, reveals an unusual constellation of signs. This commercial advertising, unexpected on the side of a religious structure, becomes even more intriguing if the "Coca-Cola, Sold Here — Ice Cold" sign is to be believed.

Rothstein's *State Line* and *Covington City Limits* were typical subjects for the photographers.

> Stryker was a great one for photographing state lines. He always wanted to see what happens when you go to one state from another. Sometimes there would be a building that would say State Line Gas Station, State Line Diner, or something like that.[9]

Both state and city lines were on the photographer's shooting script, as were movie theatres. *Gone with the Wind* had had its world premiere only two months be-fore Arthur Rothstein made his photograph of a Winchester Movie House. His caption, *Flags of the Confederacy Displayed at a Movie House on Lincoln's Birthday,* would lead us to believe that the Confederate flags were being displayed in defiance of Lincoln's birthday, but perhaps it was his unfamiliarity with the new film that caused the incongruity.

Like Arthur Rothstein, Russell Lee had been formally trained in chemistry and, like his friend Ben Shahn, took up photography to capture fleeting gestures for use in his paintings. Lee had studied painting after becoming bored with his job as a roofing plant manager. When Lee was hired, in September 1936, he was regularly making photographs of the effects of the Depression in New York City and Woodstock.

Russell Lee would often go out on the road for months at a time. His first trip, supposed to last six weeks, was nine months long. Lee would later estimate that in six years, from the time he was hired until the FSA was transferred to the OWI, he was in Washington for no more than six months. Most of that time was spent in the Midwest and West although he did travel to other areas of the country. In January 1938 he was in the Blue Ridge Mountains of Virginia and photographed a grist mill. His photographs in the file show the various details of the mechanism used to grind grain. Stryker commented about Lee's tendency to photograph in this fashion. "Russell is a taxonomist with a camera . . . he takes apart and gives you all the details." Lee worked as a photographer for the FSA longer than anyone else. He continued working for the Section after it was transferred to the OWI but later joined the Air Transport Command to aid in the nation's war effort.[10]

John Vachon
Sunday Morning
Falls Church, August 1937

John Vachon
An Ice House
Rosslyn, September 1937

John Vachon
Signs
Rosslyn, September 1937

John Vachon
A House in the Negro Quarter
Rosslyn, September 1937

John Vachon
A Sign on a Photo Studio
Fredericksburg, April 1938

John Vachon
A General Store
Diascund, October 1937

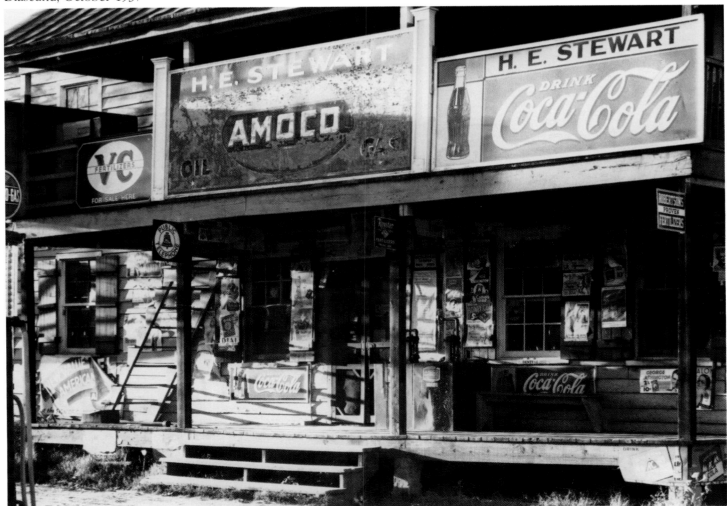

Arthur Rothstein
State Line between West Virginia and Frederick County, Virginia
February 1940

Arthur Rothstein
City Limits
Covington, January 1939

Arthur Rothstein
Gas Station Along Highway U.S. No. 50
Winchester, February 1940

Arthur Rothstein
Main Street
Winchester, February 1940

Arthur Rothstein
Flags of the Confederacy Displayed
at a Movie House on Lincoln's Birthday
Winchester, February 1940

Arthur Rothstein
Men on Main Street
Winchester, February 1940

Arthur Rothstein
A Mountain Farm; Interesting Shadows
Rappahannock County, January 1940

Arthur Rothstein
A Sign Advertising Bargain Sales on Tombstones
Lexington, January 1939

Russell Lee
Detail of Grist Mill
Near Skyline Drive, January 1938

The Tobacco Economy

Marion Post Wolcott visited the Piedmont region of Virginia in the autumns of 1939 and 1940. On one of these trips she went there to work with Sherwood Anderson on *Home Town*.[1] On both trips she photographed various aspects of the tobacco industry. Because of Stryker's economics background the FSA photographers were always obliged to document the agricultural commodities crucial to an area. To educate his photographers to the various areas of the country he encouraged them to read J. Russell Smith's socio-economic geography book *North America*. As Jack Delano was about to begin working for the FSA, Stryker sent him a letter that stressed this point:

> The main thing on which I would like for you to spend a little time is economics and geography. I recommend that you get a copy of J. Russell Smith's *North America* from the library. You may not want to read it steadily but keep it nearby and check the various sections of the country in his book.[2]

In Virginia, tobacco has been the primary money crop since John Rolfe (of Pocahontas fame) began to cultivate the "precious stink" in 1612. The topography, the rich virgin soil, and the importation of slaves in 1619 inextricably linked the economic development of Virginia with the production of tobacco.[3] Most of Virginia's tobacco has been grown in the Piedmont area. Pittsylvania County alone produced 26,609,297 pounds of tobacco in 1940, so it is with good reason that Wolcott concentrated on tobacco during her trips to that region.[4]

On October 2, 1940, Wolcott returned to Danville to make photographs of the Land Use Planning Committee. Upon her arrival she found that this was "an impossible request to make" at that time since "this is their busiest season (tobacco stripping and marketing . . .)," and thus "it would be too much to ask" for the committee to meet for a photograph. She wrote to Stryker that as an alternative she could "get a community or neighborhood land use committee meeting," and that she had "already gotten one of negroes with the county agent."[5]

Making the best of the situation, she made a series of photographs on the tobacco auction. She had arrived two weeks after the auction had begun, and tobacco was selling at $21.10 per hundred pounds, up $5.32 from the previous year. The auction would continue through mid-December, but in the first four weeks, ending October 17, 15,048,000 pounds had been sold on the Danville market.[6]

In the early 1940s Danville was the nation's primary center for handling the flue-cured bright leaf tobacco, as well as being the oldest "loose tobacco market." Traditionally, tobacco had been graded by official inspectors and sold in hogsheads, but in Danville the accepted practice became one of individual buyers inspecting the loose tobacco. Although this method of auctioning tobacco was somewhat unwieldy at first, it had evolved into an organized practice by the time Wolcott made her photographs in 1940.[7]

FSA photographers attempted to document the various aspects of any subject encountered. Thus, Marion Post Wolcott was not content to photograph only the tobacco auction itself. By photographing the farmer John D. Ferguson and his son, she included the people responsible for tobacco production. Her caption also gives some idea of what was involved in the farmers' daily routine — *They Live in Java But the Tobacco Farm Is in Nearby Chatham*. Her photograph of *A Truckload of Tobacco Being Taken to a Warehouse* records what the simple architecture lining a street in South Boston looked like. The signs on the right give the distance to Danville as twenty-nine miles and Norfolk as seventy-five miles. This provides documentation for the photograph, and of both South Boston's and Wolcott's location. Her caption *There Are Eleven Warehouses in This Small Town*, evokes a sense of the importance of the tobacco industry to South Boston.

Wolcott's caption for the photograph of Frank Petty states that he "has just had his mule shod, his corn ground, purchased some kerosene and is returning home." The services required by the farmer contrast sharply with the sign looming behind him which states "Auto Repairs: Used Parts." Certainly both mule-drawn wagons and automobiles must have been fairly common in Pittsylvania County in 1939. She recorded what, at the time, was an ordinary scene. Today the photograph can be viewed for its sense of novelty, as well as for its historical value. Wolcott writes that

> forty years ago [the photographs] were action documents calculated to transmit the reality of farm life among the lowest income and least advanced segment of the rural and farm population . . . today it is history, a collection of things as they were. . . . The viewer should be conscious of the fact that the context of the FSA photographs has changed. It is NOT the same as when it was taken forty years ago. . . .[8]

Indeed she is correct and if Roy Stryker were alive today he would probably nod his head and smile in agreement.

Marion Post Wolcott
John D. Ferguson and His Son Coming up the Road in a Tobacco Wagon;
Tobacco Barns in the Background;
They Live in Java but the Tobacco Farm is in Nearby Chatham
Java, September 1936

Marion Post Wolcott
Combination Filling Station, Garage, Blacksmith Shop, and Grocery Store;
Frank Petty, Owner of the Wagon, Has Just Had His Mule Shod, His Corn Ground,
Purchased Some Kerosene and is Returning Home
Danville, September 1939

Marion Post Wolcott
Farmers Unloading Their Tobacco from a Trailer into Baskets
the Night Before the Auction at the Hughes Warehouse
Danville, October 1940

Marion Post Wolcott
A Tobacco Auction in a Warehouse Where Many
Caswell County Farmers Sell Their Tobacco
Danville, October 1940

Marion Post Wolcott
A Farmer Waiting to Sell his Tobacco at the Auction;
The Tobacco is Piled in Baskets around Him
Danville, October 1940

Marion Post Wolcott
A Truckload of Tobacco Being Taken to a Warehouse;
There are Eleven Warehouses in this Small Town
South Boston, November 1939

Marion Post Wolcott
Sign on a Restaurant Window During Thanksgiving Week
South Boston, November 1939

Marion Post Wolcott
Loading Hay on the Ward Place
Chatham, September 1939

Marion Post Wolcott
Hog Killing on a Farm
Near Luray, November 1940

Agricultural Workers and the Norfolk-Cape Charles Ferry

In 1940 Arthur Rothstein left the Farm Security Administration to take a job with *Look* magazine. His replacement, who was living in New York City and worked as a photographer for the United Fund, was Jack Delano. Delano's salary was $2,300 a year and he had to provide his own car. Delano had studied painting and drawing at the Pennsylvania Academy of Fine Arts and had taken up photography in 1936 as a way to record his travels in Europe while on a Cresson Traveling Fellowship. In 1939 he received support from the Federal Arts Project to photographically document coal mining conditions near Pottsville, Pennsylvania. This socially conscious work, combined with his artistic training, helped Delano get a job as an FSA photographer.[1]

In May 1940, on his first excursion as an FSA photographer, Jack Delano made photographs in northern Virginia and in the southern area near Danville. He admired the artistic work of Walker Evans, and this led him to use Evans's eight-by-ten-inch view camera, even though he "had never used such a camera before." Like many beginning large-format photographers, Delano's first attempt with the camera resulted in double exposed or blank negatives. Although he thought he would be fired, Stryker jokingly told him "that even though funds were tight there was no need to economize and take two photographs on one piece of film."[2]

By late June, Delano was on Virginia's Eastern Shore following migratory workers along the Atlantic seaboard. The problems of migratory farm laborers received a great deal of public attention during the Depression. The FSA photographs made in the West, especially those by Dorothea Lange, and John Steinbeck's novel, *The Grapes of Wrath*, helped to make the severe problems of the Dust Bowl victims widely known. Compared to the West and South, Virginia had few migrant workers and most of those could be found on the Eastern Shore. A letter from Delano that arrived at the FSA office on July 2 contains a sometimes humorous and sometimes sad account of his trip:

> Unfortunately, things seemed to go wrong from the very beginning of this trip. Before I left Washington I learned from the AAA that the first Norfolk-Cape Charles ferry left at 7 a.m. So, I drove all night only to find out, at Gloucester, Virginia, that I had to take two other ferries before I got to Norfolk; which would get me to the Cape Charles ferry at 8 a.m. When I finally did get there I discovered that the first ferry left at 5 a.m! (I hope this is clear.)
>
> So I stayed around the ferry all morning watching for migrants. I spotted one car (from Florida — a small Ford with seven passengers) and photographed it and its occupants while we were waiting for the ferry. I took quite a few shots on board the ship but she was such a palatial looking steamer and all the passengers honeymooners — (except the migrants) that I'm afraid the pictures will look like ads for a travel agency![3]

Perhaps the reason Delano thought all the passengers on the ferry were honeymooners was because he had similar thoughts in mind. Delano says that "now that I had a good, steady job I figured it was time to get married." His fiancée was living in Philadelphia and she met him in Accomac so they could get married.

> We couldn't get married on July 4, it was a holiday, so we had to wait until the next day. I sent him [Stryker] a wire asking whether I could have the day off [July 5] to get married. I got a one word reply. It said "NO!" Of course, I took it to mean "don't ask idiotic questions." That was my first taste of Roy Stryker's wry humor. I was new on the job and didn't know quite how to handle him.[4]

At the time of Delano's trip, the Norfolk-Cape Charles Ferry was the only way to cross the $26\frac{1}{2}$-mile-wide mouth of the Chesapeake Bay. The ferryboat, S.S. *Princess Anne*, was indeed a "palatial looking steamer." The June 1940 *Commonwealth* described it as "the first of its kind, and the largest and fastest ferry transport in its field in the World." The ferry could accommodate between sixty and seventy-five automobiles, was constructed entirely of steel, and had quarters for both white and black truck drivers. Delano's letter continues:

> Then I came to Cheriton and found Shulkin. The first thing they told me was that the migrants had already left and for me to [go] back across the damned ferry (it takes about 2 $\frac{1}{2}$ hours to get across) toward Elizabeth. However, we did go to the canning company and I was able to get more than a close-up of barbed wire. What a place![5]

Although Delano seems somewhat insecure about his photographs on this trip, Stryker must have liked them as the series is well represented in the file, including several views of the barbed wire fence.

The series begins with the migrants waiting for the ferry at Little Creek. Delano's portrait of the migrant worker is a graceful image that shows his artistic training, as does the migrant car photograph. The shapes and shadows and three poles in the background all work together to create a harmonious composition.

Delano's photographs of the worker's living quarters on the Eastern Shore document the meager housing conditions provided by the farm owners. Even without the occupants being present we learn something about their transient way of life by seeing their personal effects. The arduous labor of workers in the onion field is emphasized in the photographs. In his notebook Delano recorded that the field hands worked from "ten to fifteen hours a day" and were paid "ten cents an hour." The workers grading cabbages were paid "twenty cents an hour."[6] His photograph of migrants playing cards offers some relief to the viewer by showing that in spite of their circumstances these people were still capable of enjoying some pleasures in life.

Jack Delano
A Farmhouse and Cane
Near Sterling, May 1940

Jack Delano
A Negro Farmer Plowing his Field of Four Acres
Near Washington, May 1940

Jack Delano
A Tenant Farmer and Some Members of His Family
in the Field Ready for Tobacco Planting
Near Danville, May 1940

Jack Delano
Cars Waiting for the Nine O'clock Ferry to Norfolk
Norfolk-Cape Charles Ferry, July 1940

Jack Delano
A Migratory Agricultural Worker Waiting for the Ferry
Norfolk-Cape Charles Ferry, July 1940

Jack Delano
A Florida Migrant's Car
Norfolk-Cape Charles Ferry, July 1940

Jack Delano
The Dock at Little Creek
Norfolk-Cape Charles Ferry, July 1940

Jack Delano
The Dock at Little Creek, the "Gateway to the South"
Norfolk-Cape Charles Ferry, July 1940

Jack Delano
Aboard the *Princess Anne* Ferryboat
Norfolk-Cape Charles Ferry, July 1940

Jack Delano
Florida Migratory Agricultural Workers Arrive
at Their New Home; There Is No Store at This Place
and the Only Drinking Water Is at the Next Farm
Near Onley, July 1940

Jack Delano
Interior of the New Home of a Group of
Florida Migrant Workers Who Have Just Arrived
Near Onley, July 1940

Jack Delano
Living Quarters to be Occupied by Migratory
Agricultural Workers during the Strawberry Season
Picket's Landing, July 1940

Jack Delano
Cooking Facilities for a Group of Thirty-five Migrant Workers
Near Onley, July 1940

Jack Delano
Florida Migrants in an Onion Field
Near Accomac, July 1940

Jack Delano
Migratory Agricultural Workers Grading Cabbages
at the Webster Canning Company
Cheriton, July 1940

Jack Delano
A Group of Migratory Agricultural Workers Playing Cards
Picket's Landing, July 1940

overleaf:
Jack Delano
Florida Migratory Worker Gathering Onions in a Field
Near Accomac, July 1940

Jack Delano
Barbed Wire Surrounded Barracks for Florida Negro
Migrants Working at the Webster Canning Company
Cheriton, July 1940

The Gold Cup Horse Race

In May 1941 Marion Post Wolcott was photographing in the Shenandoah Valley. Her assignment was to photograph the FSA housing project at Ida Valley Farms. She says that "sometimes on the weekends, when I was tired of doing projects and I felt that I deserved a little time off, I would do something recreational."[1] This was the case on Saturday, May 3, when she attended the Gold Cup Horse Race.[2]

The Virginia Gold Cup was a four-mile race, over post and rail, for horses at least four years old. On that day seventeen horses were entered in the race, which took place in front of a crowd of eight thousand spectators. In a most unusual finish, the sixth-place horse, Goldun, was declared the winner; the first five horses were all disqualified "for twice cutting a flag."[3]

Marion Post Wolcott photographed the spectators at the Gold Cup Horse Race because her "feeling was that the file was too narrow," that it was "full of Okies and dust storms." She believed that "we should be photo-graphing more of the activities of the middle class and upper middle class, and also of cities and urban scenes." She "really did feel that we needed a lot more of that kind of thing"; so she would often photograph on her own "time and those pictures would end up in the file."[4]

Wolcott's photographs do show an entirely different group of people. Consider her photograph, *Spectators at Paddock Fence*. The people sitting on the fence are all well dressed, unlike most of the people photographed by the FSA. The lady on the end, in her coat, hat, and heels, looks much too glamorous to be sitting on the roughhewn fence. It is difficult to imagine how in her attire she climbed up onto it. Another unusual scene is *Bookies Taking Bets*. The openness of the betting is surprising since horse race gambling has always been illegal in Virginia. Nonetheless, the irony of this photograph is that, while these people were wagering bets on horses, a much larger gamble was taking place with the New Deal and the ominous signs of World War II.

Marion Post Wolcott
Horses Jumping the Hurdles at the Horse Races
Warrenton, May 1941

Marion Post Wolcott
Spectators at Paddock Fence, between Races
Warrenton, May 1941

Marion Post Wolcott
Bookies Taking Bets at the Horse Races
Warrenton, May 1941

Marion Post Wolcott
Spectators at the Horse Races
Warrenton, May 1941

Marion Post Wolcott
One of the Judges at the Horse Races
Warrenton, May 1941

Defense Housing in Virginia

With the coming of World War II, the purpose of the Farm Security Administration changed. Because of the FSA's experience in providing shelter for people under the Resettlement Program, it was assigned the task of constructing housing for defense workers and for those dispossessed by the creation of military bases.

In Virginia there were two defense-related housing projects that came under the scrutiny of the Historical Section's cameras. In Radford, the construction of a gunpowder plant created an influx of thousands of workers who needed places to live. In Caroline County, the establishment of Fort A.P. Hill forced hundreds of families off their land. The Farm Security Administration was responsible for construction of new housing in both of these areas.

The Hercules Powder Plant was constructed four miles north of Radford on the New River. It consisted of more than six hundred separate buildings, dispersed for safety, on a forty-four thousand-acre site. Operating at full capacity, the plant could produce three hundred thousand pounds of smokeless powder daily and employ five thousand workers. The Hercules plant and two others under construction in Alabama and Indiana had the potential to furnish enough smokeless powder to supply an army of two million.[1]

The construction of the new plant brought jobs to Radford but it also brought problems. In November 1940 Radford's city manager reported to the Defense Housing Coordinator that "there were no vacancies at all among the 1,800 family units listed in Radford city. Three hundred of these units were termed inadequate...."[2] When thousands of men came to Radford to work, there was little to offer them in the way of housing.

President Roosevelt, on January 16, 1941, approved the construction of two hundred houses in the Radford area. One hundred twenty-nine houses were to be built in the city of Radford and seventy-one were to be constructed within twenty minutes commuting distance of the Hercules Plant. The houses in the city were constructed on a forty-acre tract and were known as Sunset Village. The two- or three-bedroom houses were to rent from twenty-one to thirty-five dollars a month.[3]

Some of the houses were located in the surrounding countryside in preparation for two eventualities. One was the fear that if too many houses were built in Radford they might become a "ghost addition" after the defense emergency passed. Secondly, because the houses were built on farms with substandard housing, the farmers would be able to buy the houses from the government after the emergency and tear down the old buildings. This was thought to be "a kind of rural slum clearance."[4]

In Caroline County seventy thousand acres were acquired to make way for the A.P. Hill Military Reservation.

> Out of the Nation's need there has come a call to the people of Caroline County, Virginia for sacrifice. The country's first Army must have an area in which it may learn in practice the lessons of modern war. So that a maneuver area may be available to troops from . . . the whole East Coast, the people of a third of Caroline County are having to leave their homes and find new places to live and work.[5]

Most of the 548 families who had to be relocated were able to leave through their own means. But for those who needed relocation assistance, the FSA constructed seventy-five four-room houses. The houses were organized in two groups of twenty-five, one group of fifteen, and another of ten. Each house was located on one acre of land to allow for a garden.

Unlike the Radford situation where there was an abundance of jobs, most of the people of Caroline County had no means of earning an income other than farming. Thus the rent, between six and eight dollars a month, was seen as a potential problem if the government had to give tenants financial assistance in order to pay their rents back to the government.[6]

By the end of 1941 more than two million acres of land had been acquired by the federal government throughout the country for army camps, airfields, and other war-related installations. This necessitated the relocation of eighteen thousand farm families onto new land. Of those, the FSA was responsible for helping more than six thousand.

The Hercules Powder Plant and Sunset Village

In November 1940 John Vachon received a promotion to junior photographer and his salary was increased to $150 a month. The next month, he drove to Radford in his newly purchased automobile to document overcrowded housing conditions caused by the influx of workers at the Hercules Powder Plant.[1] His photographs and captions tell the story of hardship imposed on both the residents of Radford and the new arrivals. The file is filled with pictures of nameless faces who had come to Radford in search of work. Vachon's captions provide the information that Stryker encouraged his photographers to collect for the historians of the future. *Men in Their Room at Mrs. Jones' Boarding House* tells the viewer that six men, who shared three beds, lived in the room and paid between eight and ten dollars rent a week although they earned only from sixty cents to $1.20 an hour. By coming to Radford, the workers had left their families behind in Bluefield, West Virginia; Bristol, Tennessee; and High Point, North Carolina. Vachon's photographs included the men who, for lack of a bed, were allowed to sit in Mr. Tilly's basement throughout the night. The photograph of three boys sleeping in the train station under a "No Loafing" sign would be humorous were it not for the sad situation it reveals.

Vachon also captured the repercussions on Radford caused by the numerous workers. The crowded bar at the Busy Bee Restaurant suggests the problems associated with a lack of entertainment for single men in a strange town. The undesirables who come in the wake of such a migration of workers is seen in *One of the New Rackets Come to Town Is Fortunetelling*. He also made the usual small-town photographs: *The Bridge into Radford, Main Street*, and people on the street *Christmas Shopping*.

Radford's new housing was photographed by John Collier in July and Marion Post Wolcott in October of 1941. The photographs show both the city project of Sunset Village and the rural housing found on *T.B. Hall's Farm*. The documentation of new housing is not as visually exciting as Vachon's earlier coverage of Radford, but Wolcott's photograph of children playing under a clothesline flapping in the breeze gives some life to the otherwise mundane assignment.

John Vachon
A Crowded Boarding House with Cars Parked Outside
Radford, December 1940

John Vachon
The Bridge into Radford;
The Hercules Powder Plant is Seven Miles Beyond the Town's Limit
Radford, December 1940

John Vachon
Men in Their Room at Mrs. Jones' Boarding House;
Six Men Live in This Room, Sleeping in Three Beds,
and Paying from Eight to Ten Dollars per Week Rent;
Most of Them Have Families They Left behind
in Bluefield, West Virginia; Bristol, Tennessee;
or High Point, North Carolina;
They Are Carpenters, Carpenter's Assistants,
Riggers, and Laborers;
They Earn from Sixty Cents to $1.25 per Hour
Radford, December 1940

John Vachon
Men Sitting around the Stove in the Basement
of Mr. Tilly's Second-hand Furniture Store;
He Allows Them to Sit Here all Night
Radford, December 1940

John Vachon
Boys from Other Places Who Have Come to Work at the Hercules
Powder Plant; They Have Been Unable to Find a Room so They are
Spending Their First Night in Town in the Railroad Station
Radford, December 1940

John Vachon
One of the New Rackets
Come to Town
Is Fortunetelling
Radford, December 1940

John Vachon
A Crowd at the Bar of the Busy Bee Restaurant
Radford, December 1940

John Vachon
Main Street
Radford, December 1940

John Vachon
Christmas Shopping
Radford, December 1940

Marion Post Wolcott
Sunset Village, Farm Security Administration
Housing Project;
Type B Homes for Defense Workers
Radford, October 1941

John Collier
A Farm Security Administration Housing Project Seen from the
Acreage of the Old Homestead Which Will Be Included in the
Expanding Home Village of the Hercules Powder Plant Workers
Radford, July 1941

Marion Post Wolcott
Sunset Village, Farm Security Administration Housing Project;
Defense Worker's Home on Carson Street
Radford, October 1941

Marion Post Wolcott
T.B. Hall's Farm, on Which the Farm Security Administration Built
a Rural Home for Defense Worker Porter C. James
Near Radford, October 1941

Fort A.P. Hill and Caroline County

By the time Jack Delano arrived in Caroline County on June 26, 1941, there were only about twenty families left to be relocated from the area being taken over by the Army.[1] His instructions were to photograph the town of Bowling Green and the new government-built housing.[2] But Delano says, "as usual with Stryker, we had complete liberty to cover everything having to do with people in those places."[3]

Delano's photographs show *The Formerly Quiet Town of Bowling Green* along with the influx of Army personnel. The postmaster of Upper Zion looks glum, perhaps because he will lose his job when the town is evacuated. Delano's photograph of a young man leaning against a Civilian Conservation Corps truck is a particularly graceful image. The boy stands as though he were a model for a painting: his head is bowed, his left arm is cocked and grasping his waist, his right arm rests on his leg, and his fingers are fully extended. The veins and muscles of his arms are revealed in minute detail. This painterly image demonstrates the influence of Delano's art background on his photography.

As can be seen in the photographs, the Civilian Conservation Corps provided assistance in moving the people into their new homes. One Caroline County woman, however, found the help offered by the Civilian Conservation Corps to be inadequate. The CCC did not want to transport her hogs to her new location. She refused their help proclaiming, "you move my all or you don't move me at all."[4]

Delano's interior photographs of a white woman and child and a black woman and her two children are examples of the equal treatment attempted by the Roosevelt administration. The sameness of the houses is striking, even down to the similar religious icons on the walls.

After his work in Caroline County was finished, Delano went to *Yorktown Beach*. The photograph of it — with families preparing the picnic table, lunching on the grass, and frolicking in the water — provides a welcome contrast to the war preparations occupying so much of the nation. This is innocent America at play before the crisis of World War II.

Jack Delano
A Field of Tobacco in the Area Being Taken Over by the Army
Caroline County, June 1941

Jack Delano
The Postmaster of Upper Zion;
When the Town Is Evacuated to Make Room for
the Army Maneuver Grounds, He Will Lose His Job
Caroline County, June 1941

The Formerly Quiet Town of Bowling Green Now Has
Huge Army Trucks Rolling Through It All Day
Caroline County, June 1941

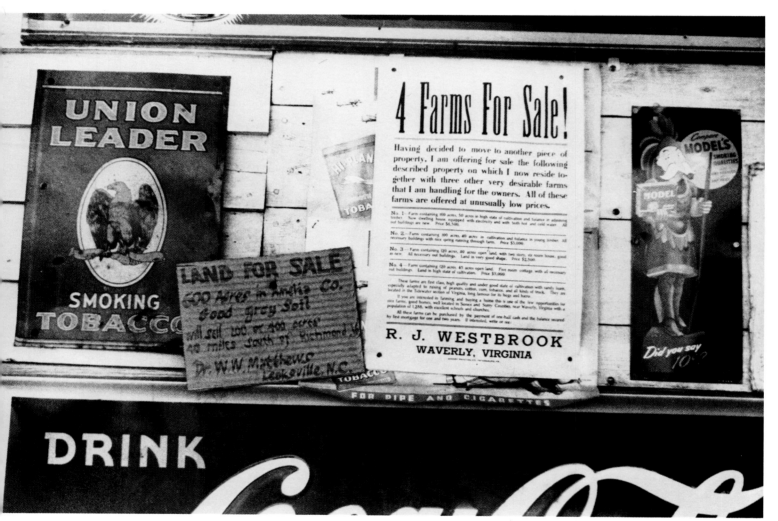

Jack Delano
Sign in a Store Near Bowling Green
Caroline County, June 1941

Jack Delano
The Owners of This Store are Planning to Move;
Most of Their Customers Have Already Moved out
of the Area Which Is Being Taken Over by the Army;
At Present Their Customers Are Mostly Soldiers
Caroline County, June 1941

Jack Delano
The Family of Russell Tombs Moving out of Their Home
Which Is in the Area Taken Over by the Army
Caroline County, June 1941

Jack Delano
Waiting for the Truck to Move Their Household Possessions
out of the Area Which Is Being Taken Over by the Army
Caroline County, June 1941

Jack Delano
Pre-fabricated Houses Built by the Farm Security Administration to House Some of
the Negro Farmers Who Had to Move from Their Houses When the Area Was
Taken Over by the Army for Maneuver Grounds
Caroline County, June 1941

upper right:
Jack Delano
This Woman and Her Family Moved from the Area Taken Over by the
Army to a Pre-fabricated House Built by the Farm Security Administration
to House Some of the People Forced out of Their Homes
Caroline County, June 1941

page 112:
Jack Delano
Civilian Conservation Corps Trucks Are Helping
This Young Man's Family Move Their Belongings
out of the Area Being Taken Over by the Army
Caroline County, June 1941

lower right:
Jack Delano
This Family Had to Move out of the Area Being Taken Over by the
Army for Maneuver Grounds; They Are Now Living in One of the
Pre-fabricated Houses Built by the Farm Security Administration
for These People
Caroline County, June 1941

Hampton Roads and Defense

John Vachon visited Hampton Roads in March 1941 to document the effects of the defense buildup on the area. Because of its extensive shipbuilding facilities, strategic location at the mouth of the Chesapeake Bay and center of the East Coast, and as the point of command for the Navy's Atlantic operations, Hampton Roads experienced dynamic growth prior to and during the Second World War. The problem was not solely one of workers seeking employment. The stationing of thousands of naval personnel at the area's military installations coupled with the influx of those wishing to visit the sailors magnified the problem. It was estimated that by November 1941 the population of Norfolk had doubled since the defense movement began three years earlier.[1] Vachon's instructions were to emphasize the strain placed on housing and health facilities caused by the migration of people into the area. Specifically he was to show such things as out-of-state license plates on the cars of workers. Generally he was "to stress the renewed rural to urban migration, the pull of defense centers on the 'dammed-up' rural people of the '30s." The government was consciously attempting to record the shift of people from rural to urban.[2]

Vachon arrived in Hampton Roads during the middle of March and stayed at the Southland Hotel in Norfolk and the Hotel Warwick in Newport News.[3] His photographs, made in Norfolk, Portsmouth, and Newport News, document existing housing conditions, trailer camps, and the role of community service organizations in providing shelter to the thousands of migrants. Of course he also made the usual FSA photographs. Views of Main Street, the vanishing profession of iceman, and a newsstand give some of the particulars which made up the changing culture of Hampton Roads in 1941.

But the aim of his trip, to record the problems of overcrowded housing, does not provide a pleasant view. In Norfolk and Portsmouth the starkness of the area surrounding the plain frame houses gives the impression of a drab existence. The interior photographs reveal poor living conditions. The numerous trailer camps that sprang up to house workers are also documented. Following instructions, Vachon included out-of-state license plates to document the origins of the workers. His photograph of a Norfolk trailer camp includes a scene familiar to residents of the area, the "Southern Belle" Roller Coaster.[4]

The Helping Hand Mission in Portsmouth and the Salvation Army in Newport News are both well represented in the file. Although both were within Vachon's official area of concern, he seems to have become intrigued by them. His photograph of *Men Eating at the Salvation Army* provides a humorous comparison between the dour-looking man on the right and the man on the left who seems intent on devouring a stack of sliced bread. *The Mission Pianist in his Room at the Helping Hand Mission* is a bizarre sociological study. The pianist sits in a room cluttered with a dizzying array of wires, oblivious to his surroundings. Besides the watch on his arm he has two clocks on the mantel, each with a different time.

Vachon's photograph of men leaving the shipyard is shot from the same high vantage point that Paul Carter used five years earlier when he visited Newport News. Carter's caption states that seven thousand men were employed in 1936. By the time Vachon visited the area, nearly seventeen thousand men were working three shifts with thousands more workers to be added. The photograph and text, together, document the dramatic increases in population being experienced in the area.[5]

John Vachon
Ice and Icicles
Harrisonburg, January 1941

John Vachon
A Used Car Garage
Bedford, March 1941

John Vachon
Paper Mill
West Point, March 1941

John Vachon
Court Day; The Eye of God, Surrounded by a Glory,
on the Wall behind the Judge's Seat
Rustburg, March 1941

Paul Carter
Men Coming from Work at the Shipyard;
This Yard Employs Approximately Seven Thousand Men
Newport News, September 1936

overleaf:
John Vachon
An Episcopal Church by the Roadside
King William County, March 1941

John Vachon
The Four O'clock Shift Leaving the Shipyard
at the End of Their Work Period
Newport News, March 1941

John Vachon
A Man Who Is Staying at the Salvation Army
Newport News, March 1941

John Vachon
Men Eating at the Salvation Army
Newport News, March 1941

John Vachon
The Mission Pianist in his Room at the Helping Hand Mission
Portsmouth, March 1941

John Vachon
The Helping Hand Mission;
Taking the Collection
Portsmouth, March 1941

John Vachon
The Family of a Defense Worker from North Carolina;
They Live in a One-room Apartment in the Helping Hand Mission
Portsmouth, March 1941

John Vachon
Courthouse Square
Portsmouth, March 1941

John Vachon
Houses Near the Navy Yard;
Rent is Four Dollars per Month
Portsmouth, March 1941

John Vachon
Houses near the Navy Yard
Portsmouth, March 1941

John Vachon
The Front Porch of a Rooming House
Portsmouth, March 1941

John Vachon
Children of Construction Workers
Portsmouth, March 1941

John Vachon
A Trailer Camp for Defense Workers
Norfolk, March 1941

John Vachon
A Construction Worker and His Family
Who Are Living at a Trailer Camp
Portsmouth, March 1941

John Vachon
Four O'clock Traffic
[Indian River and Wilson Roads]
Norfolk, March 1941

John Vachon
A Backed-up Sewer in the Negro Slum District
Norfolk, March 1941

John Vachon
Housing
Norfolk, March 1941

John Vachon
Housing
Norfolk, March 1941

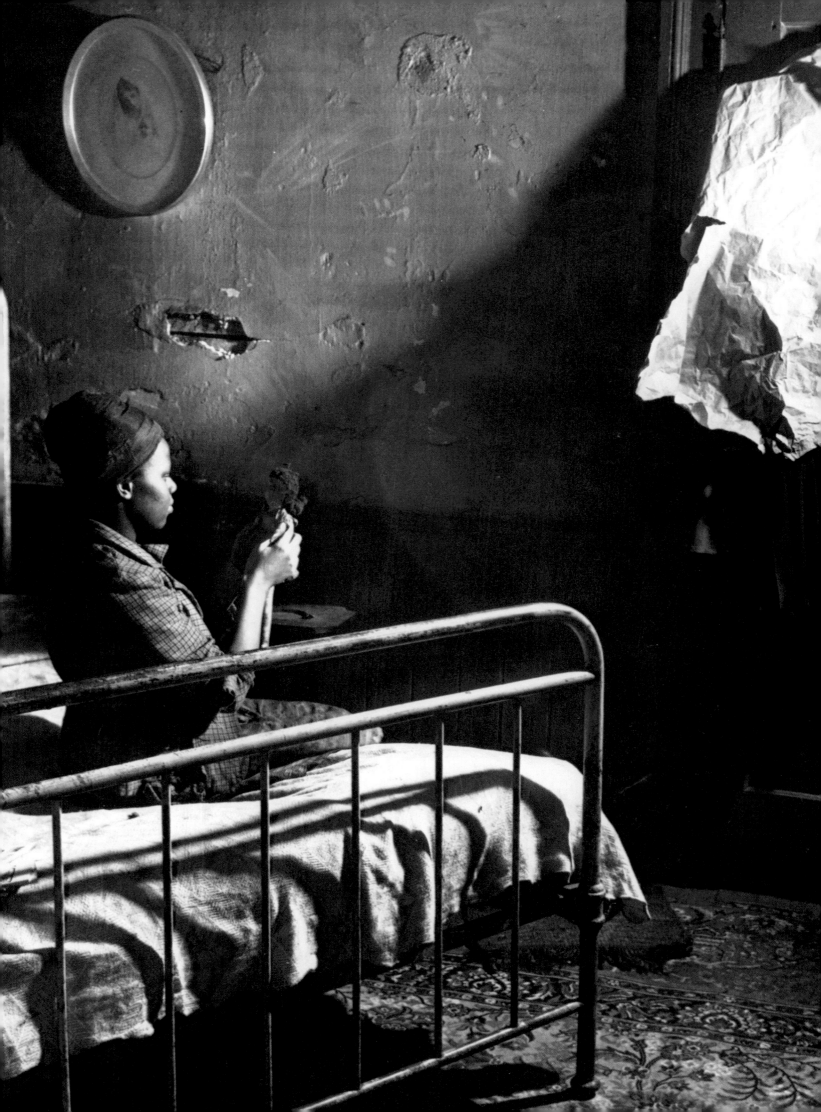

John Vachon
An Iceman
Norfolk, March 1941

overleaf:
John Vachon
A Bedroom in a House in the Negro Slum District
Norfolk, March 1941

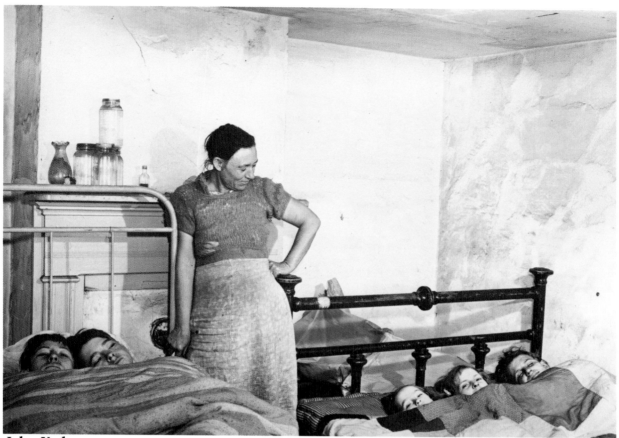

John Vachon
A Mother and Some of Her Children; They Came from a North Carolina Farm in order that
Her Husband and Older Sons Might Get Employment in Defense Industries
Norfolk, March 1941

John Vachon
A Defense Worker and His Family;
They Came from North Carolina and Are at Present Living in a One-room Apartment
Portsmouth, March 1941

John Vachon
A Newsstand
Norfolk, March 1941

The Irony of Accomplishment

The success of the Historical Section can be measured by the frequency with which its photographs were used. By publishing the photographs — in pamphlets, magazines, and books — and presenting them in exhibitions, the Section was doing its job of making people aware of the problems of rural poverty. *Look* and *Survey Graphic* frequently made use of the images as did many other magazines. The photographs were used for government publications such as annual reports and pamphlets.[1] *U.S. Camera Annual* featured the photographs regularly; the 1938 issue devoted thirty-two pages to FSA photographs. They were given lavish exposure in 1938 because they were highly praised in the *International Photographic Exhibition*, held that spring at the Grand Central Palace in New York. By publishing the photographs, *U.S. Camera* gave the photographs a wider audience. Edwin Rosskam was responsible for the organization of many government-sponsored exhibitions which travelled around the country.[2] In 1936 the College Art Association organized a travelling exhibition of 110 photographs. In 1939 Dorothea Lange had published her book, a collaboration with Paul Taylor, titled *American Exodus*. Other books included Sherwood Anderson's *Home Town*, 1940; *Land of the Free*, 1938 (an unusual work that Archibald MacLeish described as a book of poems about the photographs); *Roots of America: A Travelogue of American Personalities*, 1936, by Charles Morrow Wilson; *Twelve Million Black Voices: A Folk History of the Negro in the United States*, 1941, by Richard Wright and Edwin Rosskam; and *Poems of the Midwest*, 1946, by Carl Sandburg. *Virginia: A Guide to the Old Dominion* was one of forty separate state guides published by the Federal Writers Project of the Works Progress Administration which used FSA photographs. The Writers Project also published five other regional and ethnic guides such as *The Negro in Virginia*, 1940.

The Historical Section's reputation for producing good quality work was well established both within the government and in the public eye. The unit was receiving wide acclaim by the time World War II began for America. However, the functioning of the agency became harder to maintain amid the changing political climate in Washington. To make his photographic services indispensable Stryker frequently did work for other government agencies. The Office of War Information was a frequent customer, and in September 1942 the Historical Section was completely transferred to that agency.

The business of the OWI was of a decidedly propagandistic nature. Because of this, its photographs generally seem stilted beside the earlier work of the Historical Section. The photographs, reproduced in war-related magazines and leaflets, were intended to stir feelings of patriotism. The idealism of using photography for social change and to support New Deal Programs was no longer necessary.

Gordon Parks's photographs of Constantine P. Lihas, a Greek-American soldier, can be used to illustrate the type of work undertaken by the OWI. Lihas, whose parents were Greek immigrants, is doing his part to aid in the nation's war effort. An individual with a Greek background emphasizes the melting pot heritage of America where a new breed of people banded together to fight a common enemy. The photographs are intended to symbolize the unity that Americans were supposed to feel during the war.

Gordon Parks can also be used to illustrate the fame that the Historical Section was experiencing at this time. While working as a railroad porter, Parks had become familiar with FSA photographs in magazines. He had met Jack Delano, who encouraged him to apply for a Julius Rosenwald Fellowship. Parks used the two hundred dollars a month provided by the fellowship to work under the direction of Roy Stryker. He began work in January 1942 as a volunteer photographer in the Historical Section.[3]

By this time Stryker's sphere of influence was considerable. Others, such as Marjory Collins, Martha MacMillan, Andreas Feininger, Arthur Siegel, and Esther Bubley worked both as staff and non-staff photographers. Even though there were more photographers under Stryker, the demands of the war effort left little time to make the memorable photographs of the FSA's earlier years. The nature of the work became primarily war propaganda, and the documentation of Americans suffering through the Depression turned into a record of the country's mobilization for war.

By the time John Collier joined the staff in the summer of 1941, there was little opportunity to engage in the small-town documentaries. Collier had studied painting at the California School of Fine Arts. A childhood friend, Dorothea Lange, sparked his interest in photography.[4]

In Virginia, Collier did an extensive documentation of Martin Auto Body in Arlington. His photographs show the myriad of activities that takes place in reconditioning auto bodies. Two of his photographs from that series are included in this section. The exterior view of the shop gives the setting and provides a contrast between the automobile and the outmoded horse-drawn carriage. His *Patriotic License Tag Slogan* gives the essence of the American spirit of May 1942: "Let's Bury The Axis: We Are Ready, America, To Do Our Part." The country was rallying to win the war and Collier captured that spirit in a small detail. As Stryker had said, it is the particulars which taken together make up our culture.

With the exception of Stryker, John Vachon was with the Historical Section longer that anyone else. By March and June of 1943 (his last trips to Virginia) the work was mostly propaganda for the OWI. But Vachon seems to have been able to slip into the file a few of the photographs for which the Section was so well known. His Lynchburg photographs, included in this catalogue, are quite modern in spirit. In these, Vachon reveals a greatly refined sense of design. Although the photographs include some prerequisite signs, form is more of a consideration than content. This is, of course, not in keeping with the documentary concept in which content is the primary concern.

The final photograph considered here is Vachon's June 1943 Harrisonburg view, a fitting close to this study. The *Honor Role of Men in the Armed Services* confirms the country's involvement in, and commitment to, the war. Vachon's rise through the ranks of the Historical Section parallels the growth of documentary photography as a genre during this eight-year period. When the Resettlement Administration began, both documentary photography and Vachon were young and impressionable. The

potential of the medium and of the man could not have been forseen in 1935. It took practical experience and intellectual consideration to define the missions of the two. They both began without established direction and finished with a strong understanding of what the documentary photographer could achieve.

By 1943 World War II was raging in Europe and in the Pacific. The Historical Section's work under the Office of War Information was solely propaganda and Stryker's position had been reduced to little more than that of an administrator. The photographs in the file, over seven years of work, were in danger. The Office of War Information was managed by a former Associated Press man. The Associated Press staff had always been opposed to the FSA work and would have been glad to see the entire file destroyed. There were similar feelings within Congress. Without the knowledge of his superiors at the OWI, Stryker negotiated the transfer of the FSA photographs to the Library of Congress. There the file was safe and has remained to this day. Stryker resigned from government service on October 2, 1943. He went on to direct a similar photographic project for Standard Oil of New Jersey showing how petroleum affects our lives.[5]

John Collier
Auto Body Work Plant;
Patriotic License Tag Slogan Advertising
Arlington, May 1942

John Collier
Auto Body Work Plant
Arlington, May 1942

John Collier
Blue Ridge Farm Security Administration Farm Labor Camp
Timberville, September 1942

Gordon Parks
Constantine P. Lihas,
in the Middle on the Far Side,
at Noon Mess
Fort Belvoir, December 1942

Gordon Parks
Constantine P. Lihas in Gas Mask
and Decontamination Suit
Fort Belvoir, December 1942

Gordon Parks
Constantine P. Lihas, a Twenty-one-year Old
Greek American Soldier, Formerly a Material
Handler at the General Electric Company Plant
in Pittsburgh; Both Parents were Born in
Greece; Father Came to the United States in
1906, Mother in 1921; He Was Born in This
Country and Has Been in the Army for Five
Months
Fort Belvoir, December 1942

Gordon Parks
Constantine P. Lihas in the
Top Turret of a Tank
Fort Belvoir, December 1942

149

Marjory Collins
Farm Security Administration Trailer Camp Project for Negroes;
General View of the Project
from the Roof of the Community Building
Arlington, April 1942

Marjory Collins
Farm Security Administration Trailer Camp Project for Negroes;
Project Occupant Tending His Victory Garden
Arlington, April 1942

John Vachon
A Barber in Front of His Shop
Lynchburg, March 1943

John Vachon
In Front of the Hotel Carroll
Lynchburg, March 1943

John Vachon
A Truck Driver at the Terminal, Waiting to Go Out
Lynchburg, March 1943

John Vachon
Honor Roll of Men in the Armed Services
at the County Court House
Harrisonburg, June 1943

A Humanistic Consideration

In 1839, William Henry Fox Talbot wrote about his new invention of photography: "it renders with the utmost truth and fidelity."[1] This ability to record a scene or subject in intricate detail and with complete veracity at the instant of exposure makes photography a unique device. Because of this it was immediately and widely used as a means to document subjects or events. Some prominent examples are photographs of the Civil War by Matthew Brady and others, Carleton Watkins's views of Yosemite, and Eugène Atget's images of Paris.

In the nineteenth century and during the Depression, the United States Government frequently exploited photography's potential. Photographers were employed to accompany survey parties exploring the vast, unknown American West as early as 1866.[2] During the 1930s, 70 percent of all New Deal agencies used photography in some way.[3] However, none had the considerable scope of the Historical Section nor did they employ such talented photographers.

In 1889 *The British Journal of Photography* advocated the formation of an archive of photographs recording "the present state of the world" and noted that "these will be most valuable documents a century hence."[4] Because a photograph is considered truthful, it is allowed to stand as proof of an original's existence. This act of documentation is an intrinsic part of the photographic process.

The FSA photographs were the first to be called documentary.[5] A recognized genre, documentary photography depicts the real world with the intention of making a comment. This definition concedes that photography is not a completely honest medium. The integrity of the photograph is compromised because it is made by an individual who, naturally, has a bias. Thus it cannot be an objective viewpoint.

John Grierson (although writing about film) was the first to use the word "documentary" in a commentary sense.[6] He was opposed to the make-believe films of Hollywood; he believed films should be made of real life. In film, Grierson looked for "what actually moves: what hits the spectator at the midriff: what yanks him up by the hair of the head or the plain bootstraps to the plane of decent seeing."[7] Edward Steichen, writing about the FSA photographers in *U.S. Camera 1939*, noted, "these documents told stories and told them with such simple and blunt directness that they made many a citizen wince."[8] The power of documentary that Grierson and Steichen were trying to describe was not merely the information-giving ability of photography, but the capacity of the imagery to move the viewer. The photograph easily provides factual information, but to be effective, the image must be *felt* — this, then, is the essence of documentary photography.[9]

Documentary photography has become generally associated with the concern for recording human conditions. Jacob Riis was the first in the United States to use photographs to change social conditions. Riis, a Danish immigrant, was a police reporter for *The New York Herald*. Riis wanted to help European immigrants living in overcrowded tenements in New York City. He began by writing articles about the poor conditions, but soon realized that to make the maximum impression on others he needed to show the miserable conditions graphically. To this purpose, Riis learned photography to produce irrefutable evidence of what he wrote. In 1890, he published *How the Other Half Lives: Studies Among the Tenements of New York*. The book provided a factual account in words and photographs of the disgraceful conditions endured by the poor.[10]

More effective than the pioneering efforts of Riis was the work of Lewis Hine. Ben Shahn said, "Hine was one of the Greats. I don't know a photographer who has not been conscious of, and influenced to some extent by, Lewis Hine."[11] Hine began photographing immigrants on Ellis Island in 1905. He photographed life in the slums and sweatshops of New York and in 1908 was employed by the National Child Labor Committee. He then concentrated on photographing children who were forced to work long hours, often under unsafe conditions, in the nation's factories and fields. They were widely published in magazines, pamphlets, and books, and were instrumental in the passage of child labor laws. Hine explained his motivation when he said, "I wanted to show the things that had to be corrected; I wanted to show the things that had to be appreciated."[12]

Lewis Hine called his imagery advocating social improvement "photo-interpretations." Photography that attempts to understand and reveal the state of humanity has been called many things. "Documentary" was used to describe the FSA photographs because it was a new term in the 1930s and it seemed to suit the work. Occasionally, the phrase "social-documentary" has been used to describe the work of Hine, Riis, and the FSA.

Dorothea Lange and Beaumont Newhall together grappled with the inadequacy of the term "documentary" to describe photographs dealing with the human condition. They rejected "historical" because it seemed to exclude the present, and they thought "factual" was too cold because it did not take into account the ability of a photograph to attract the viewer back repeatedly.[13]

Walker Evans thought that "documentary" was a "sophisticated and misleading word." He believed the term should be "documentary-style." He explained, "a document has use, whereas art is really useless. Therefore art is never a document, though it certainly can adopt that style."[14] Cornell Capa, in his books and exhibitions, used the term "Concerned Photographer" to explain "the unique artistic creations and documentary/commentary depictions of the world in which we live."[15]

Recently, Beaumont Newhall has suggested a new, and what this author believes to be more appropriate, name for photography concerned with the human condition: "Humanistic."[16] Although broader in locution, "humanistic" is more accurate in describing the concern of this kind of photograph. Humanistic is defined as an "attitude centered on human interests or values; especially a philosophy that asserts the dignity and worth of man and his capacity for self-realization through reason."[17]

The FSA photographs do not pity or mock their subjects. Invariably, they show the nobility of people who, through no fault of their own, must endure unfortunate circumstances. Roy Stryker said:

> But most important, there is in this collection an attitude toward people. To my knowledge there is no picture in there that in any way whatsoever represents an attempt by a photographer to ridicule his subject, to be cute with him, to violate his privacy, or to do something to make a cliché . . . our photographers had one thing in common, and that was a deep respect for human beings. There's honesty there, and compassion, and a natural regard for individual dignity.[18]

The FSA photographers were most concerned with documenting the conditions of Americans during the Depression; thus their work clearly falls within the domain of humanistic photography. Arthur Rothstein made a statement in 1964 that further affirms the accuracy of "humanistic photography" as descriptive of the FSA's work:

> I think we had a great social responsibility. We were dedicated to the idea that our lives can be improved, that man is the master of his environment and that it is possible for us to live a better life, not only materially, but spiritually as well. . . . There was a missionary sense of dedication to this project — of making the world a better place in which to live.[19]

This discussion has considered the origins of, and the unwillingness to accept, the cold, scientific term "documentary" to describe what some would call art. This author suggests that "humanistic" is indeed a more appropriate term, as humanistic succinctly describes the photographic work by the Farm Security Administration.

Notes

Introduction

[1] Sidney Baldwin, *Poverty and Politics: The Rise and Decline of the Farm Security Administration* (Chapel Hill: The University of North Carolina Press, 1968), pp. 128, 187.

[2] F. Jack Hurley, *Portrait of a Decade* (Baton Rouge: Louisiana State University Press, 1972), p. 164.

[3] Roy E. Stryker and Paul H. Johnstone, "Documentary Photographs," in *The Cultural Approach to History,* ed. Caroline F. Ware (New York: Columbia University Press, 1940), p. 328.

[4] Roy E. Stryker, Interview, Montrose Colorado, October 17, 1963, Roy Stryker Papers, Photographic Archives, University of Louisville, Louisville, Kentucky.

[5] Within each of the regional groups there are twelve subject headings: Land; Towns and Cities; People; Home; Transportation; Agriculture, Fishing and Mining; Business and Engineering; Manufacturing and Processing; Government and Politics; War, Armed Forces; Medicine, Religion, Education; and Social Activities. These sections are further divided into a total of thirteen hundred subheadings. Under the subject heading of People, for example, there are fifty-four subheadings such as Youths, Men in Their Prime, Middle-Aged Men, and Old Men.

[6] Although incomplete, most of the photographs can be seen in their original sequence on microfilm at the Library of Congress.

[7] Rexford Tugwell's decision to use photography to sell the Resettlement Administration Programs to the country was only one aspect of a larger public relations effort. The Historical Section was one of five parts of what was known as the Information Division. The other sections were: the Editorial Section, to inform the general public about the activities of the Resettlement Administration; the Publication Section, to provide information about the activities to magazines and other publications; the Radio Section, to disseminate information; and the Documentary Film Section.

[8] "Documentary Photographs From the Files of the Resettlement Administration: A College Art Association Exhibition," Roy Stryker Papers.

[9] Franklin Delano Roosevelt, *Selected Speeches, Press Conferences, and Letters,* Ed. Basil Rauch (New York, 1957), cited by William Stott, *Documentary Expression and Thirties America* (New York: Oxford University Press, 1973), p. 26.

The Synthesis of the Section

[1] Personnel Record, Roy Stryker Papers.

[2] Nancy Wood, *In This Proud Land: America 1935-1943 As Seen In the FSA Photographs* (New York: Galahad Books, 1973), p. 12.

[3] Karin Becker Ohrn, *Dorothea Lange and the Documentary Tradition* (Baton Rouge: Louisiana State University Press, 1980), pp. 46-47.

[4] Ohrn, p. 109-236.

[5] Walker Evans, "Walker Evans, Visiting Artist," in *Photography: Essay and Images,* ed. Beaumont Newhall (New York: Museum of Modern Art, 1980), pp. 315-317.

[6] Hank O'Neal, *A Vision Shared: A Classic Portrait of America and Its People, 1935-1943* (New York: St. Martin's Press, 1976), p. 60.

[7] Lincoln Kirstein, *Walker Evans: American Photographs* (New York: Museum of Modern Art, 1938), p. 178.

[8] Leslie Katz, "An Interview with Walker Evans," in *Photography in Print: Writings from 1816 to the Present,* ed. Vicki Goldberg (New York: Simon and Schuster, 1981), p. 363.

[9] Hurley, *Portrait of a Decade,* p. 50; Roy E. Stryker, Interview, Roy Stryker Papers.

A New Deal in Housing

[1] Roy Stryker Papers.

[2] Paul K. Conkin, *Tomorrow a New World: The New Deal Community Program* (Ithaca: Cornell University Press, 1959), p. 7.

[3] Conkin, p. 240.

[4] Conkin, p. 110.

[5] J.R. Lassiter, "Shenandoah National Park," *The Commonwealth,* July 1936, p. 10.

[6] Lassiter, p. 10.

[7] Carolyn and Jack Reeder, *Shenandoah Heritage: The Story of the People Before the Park* (Washington, D.C.: The Potomac Appalachian Trail Club, 1978), p. 39.

[8] Scott Shelton, "The Shenandoah National Park: Its Impact on a Mountain People" (M.A. Thesis, Old Dominion University, Norfolk, Virginia, 1984), p. 15.

[9] October 8, 1936, Department of Agriculture, Farm Security Administration, Record Group 96, National Archives, Washington, D.C., cited by Conkin, p. 163.

[10] Washington *Star,* May 27, 1937; Harry F. Byrd to Henry A. Wallace, Congressional Record, 75th Congress, 1st Session, 1937, pp. 7964-7967, cited by Conkin, p. 164.

[11] "Shenandoah Homesteads: Final Report of Project Costs to June 30, 1939," National Archives, cited by Conkin, p. 164.

[12] Conkin, p. 200.

[13] "Newport News Homesteads," National Archives.

[14] Ronald L. Heinemann, *Depression and New Deal in Virginia: The Enduring Dominion* (Charlottesville: University Press of Virginia, 1983), p. 123.

The Dispossessed of the Blue Ridge

[1] Arthur Rothstein, Interview, New Rochelle, N.Y., January 17, 1985; Arthur Rothstein, *Arthur Rothstein: Words and Pictures* (New York: American Photographic Book Publishing Co., 1979), pp. 6-7.

[2] Rothstein, Interview.

[3] Rothstein, Interview.

[4] Rothstein, Interview.

[5] Rothstein, Interview.

[6] Rothstein, Interview.

[7] Rothstein, *Words and Pictures,* p. 7.

[8] Ida Valley Farms, in Page County, was one of seven separate projects that together were known as Shenandoah Homesteads. The others were Elkton and Hensley in Rockingham County, C.I.B. School in Greene County, Wolftown and Madison in Madison County, and Flint Hill in Rappahannock County.

[9] Hurley, *Portrait of a Decade,* p. 110.

[10] Shelton, pp. 47-48.

Aberdeen Gardens and Newport News

[1] Hurley, *Portrait of a Decade,* p. 76.

[2] O'Neal, p. 267.

[3] John Vachon, "Tribute to a Man, an Era, an Art," *Harper's,* September 1973, pp. 96-97; *Just Before the War,* comp. Thomas H. Garver (Balboa, California: Newport Harbor Art Museum, 1968), p. 9.

[4] Vachon, "Tribute," pp. 96-97; *Just Before the War,* p. 9.

[5] Rothstein, Interview.

[6] Vachon, "Tribute," p. 97.

The Small Town Aesthetic

[1] Vachon, "Tribute," p. 97.

[2] Vachon, "Tribute," p. 97.

[3] *Middletown* was an in-depth sociological study of an average American town; Robert and Helen M. Lynd, *Middletown: A Study in American Culture* (New York: Harcourt, Brace and Company, Inc., 1929).

[4] Roy E. Stryker in *Just Before the War*, p. 14; Hurley, *Portrait of a Decade*, pp. 96, 98-100.

[5] "The Farm Security Photographer Covers the Small Town," Roy Stryker Papers.

[6] Carole Rifkind, *Main Street: The Face of Urban America* (New York: Harper and Row, Publishers, Inc., 1977), pp. 63-73.

[7] Wood, p. 8.

[8] David D. Ryan, "Sherwood Anderson's Hideaway in the Hills," *Commonwealth*, January 1981, p. 37.

[9] Rothstein, Interview.

[10] F. Jack Hurley, *Russell Lee: Photographer*, (Dobbs Ferry: Morgan and Morgan, Inc., 1978) p. 14; O'Neal, p. 136.

The Tobacco Economy

[1] Marion Post Wolcott, Letter, March 17, 1985.

[2] Roy E. Stryker to Jack Delano, March 1, 1940, Roy Stryker Papers.

[3] Virginius Dabney, *Virginia: The New Dominion* (Charlottesville: The University Press of Virginia, 1971), pp. 24-25.

[4] Roy Wood, "Farm Tenancy in Virginia" (M.A. Thesis, University of Virginia, 1948), p. 42.

[5] Marion Post Wolcott to Roy E. Stryker, October 2, 1940, Roy Stryker Papers.

[6] Clarence W. Newman, Ed., "Business Inventory," *The Commonwealth*, November 1940, p. 3.

[7] Glen Scanlan, "Marketing Tobacco in Danville," *The Commonwealth*, November 1940, p. 11.

[8] Marion Post Wolcott, Letter.

Agricultural Workers and the Norfolk-Cape Charles Ferry

[1] O'Neal, p. 234.

[2] O'Neal, p. 234.

[3] Jack Delano to Roy Stryker, July 2, 1940, Roy Stryker Papers.

[4] Jack Delano, Interview, March 15, 1985.

[5] Jack Delano to Roy Stryker.

[6] Delano, Interview.

The Gold Cup Horse Race

[1] Marion Post Wolcott, Interview, March 14, 1985.

[2] Richmond *Times Dispatch*, May 3, 1941, p. 1.

[3] Richmond *Times Dispatch*, May 3, 1941, p. 15; Richmond *Times Dispatch*, May 4, 1941, Section II, p. 1.

[4] Wolcott, Interview.

Defense Housing in Virginia

[1] Smokeless powder is not of the exploding variety, such as TNT, but is, instead, a propellant used to launch bullets and cannon shells, Clarence W. Newman, "Powder Output Begins at Radford," *The Commonwealth*, April 1941, p. 7.

[2] "Defense Housing — Radford and Pulaski, Virginia," December 5, 1941, National Archives.

[3] *FSA Annual Report*, 1941, p. 25, National Archives.

[4] *FSA Annual Report*, p. 15.

[5] Grant McConnell to John Fischer, July 3, 1941, National Archives.

[6] Grant McConnell to John Fischer.

The Hercules Powder Plant and Sunset Village

[1] Vachon, "Tribute," p. 95.

Fort A.P. Hill and Caroline County

[1] Grant McConnell to John Fischer.

[2] Roy Stryker, Ned Trapnell, John Fischer, Jack Bryan, Telephone Conversation, June 25, 1941, Roy Stryker Papers.

[3] Delano, Interview.

[4] Grant McConnell to John Fischer.

Hampton Roads and Defense

[1] Thomas J. Wertenbaker, *Norfolk: Historic Southern Port* (Durham, North Carolina: Duke University Press, 1962), p. 347.

[2] F.P. Weber to Roy E. Stryker, March 3, 1941, Roy Stryker Papers.

[3] John Vachon to Roy E. Stryker, March 15, 1941, Roy Stryker Papers.

[4] Built in 1900, the mile-long thriller was ignominiously blown up in the 1979 movie, *The Death of Ocean View Park*.

[5] Parke Rouse, Jr., "Newport News and Defense," *The Commonwealth*, June 1941, p. 11.

The Irony of Accomplishment

[1] Penelope Dixon, *Photographers of the Farm Security Administration: An Annotated Bibliography, 1930-1980* (New York: Garland Publishing, Inc., 1983), pp. 211-218.

[2] Hurley, *Portrait of a Decade*, p. 144.

[3] Gordon Parks, Lecture, International Center of Photography, New York, November 17, 1984; Martin H. Bush, *The Photographs of Gordon Parks* (Kansas: Edwin A. Ulrich Museum of Art, Witchita State University, 1983), p. 36.

[4] O'Neal, p. 267.

[5] Hurley, *Portrait of a Decade*, p. 144.

A Humanistic Consideration

[1] William Henry Fox Talbot, "Some Account of the Art of Photogenic Drawing," in *Photography in Print*, ed. Goldberg, p. 39.

[2] Weston J. Naef and James N. Wood, *Era of Exploration: The Rise of Landscape Photography in the American West, 1860-1885* (New York: Albright-Knox Art Gallery, The Metropolitan Museum of Art, 1975), p. 50.

[3] James L. McCamy, *Government Publicity: Its Practice in Federal Administration* (Chicago, 1939), p. 233, cited in Hurley, *Portrait of a Decade*, p. viii.

[4] Beaumont Newhall, *The History of Photography: From 1839 to the Present* (New York: The Museum of Modern Art, 1982), p. 235.

[5] Richard L. Williams, ed., *Documentary Photography*, Life Library of Photography (New York: Time-Life Books, 1972), p. 66.

6 Reviewing Robert Flaherty's *Moana* for the New York *Sun* in February 1926, Grierson wrote "being a visual account of events in the daily life of a Polynesian youth, has documentary value." The word came from the French *documentaire* and was used to describe travel films. Grierson would later define the term as "the creative treatment of actuality." Forsyth Hardy, ed., *Grierson on Documentary* (New York: Praeger Publishers, 1966), p. 13.

7 Hardy, p. 42.

8 Edward Steichen, "The FSA Photographers," in *Essays and Images*, ed. Newhall, p. 267.

9 Stott, pp. 11-12.

10 Naomi Rosenblum, *A World History of Photography* (New York: Abbeville Press, Inc., 1984), p. 359.

11 Judith Mara Gutman, *Lewis W. Hine and the American Social Conscience* (New York: Walker and Company, 1967), pp. 2, 60.

12 Arthur Siegel, "Fifty Years of Documentary," in *Photographers on Photography*, ed. Nathan Lyons (Englewood Cliffs, New Jersey: Prentice-Hall, Inc., 1966), p. 90.

13 Beaumont Newhall, *Dorothea Lange Looks at the American Country Woman* (Fort Worth, Texas: Amon Carter Museum, 1967), p. 5.

14 Leslie Katz, p. 364.

15 Cornell Capa, ed., *The Concerned Photographer 2* (New York: Grossman Publishers, 1972), np.

16 Beaumont Newhall, "A Backward Glance at Documentary," in *Observations: Essays on Documentary Photography*, ed. David Featherstone (Carmel, California: Friends of Photography, 1984), p. 2.

17 Webster's New Collegiate Dictionary, 1981 ed., s.v. humanism.

18 Wood, p. 7.

19 Rothstein, *Words and Pictures*, pp. 7, 8; Arthur Rothstein, Interview, New York, May 25, 1964, Archives of American Art, Washington D.C., p. 19.

Bibliography

Allen, Frederick Lewis. *Since Yesterday: The Nineteen-Thirties in America.* New York and London: Harper and Brothers Publishers, 1940.

The American Studies Association. *American Perspectives: The National Self-Image in the Twentieth Century.* Cambridge: Harvard University Press, 1961.

Anderson, James C., ed. *Roy Stryker: The Humane Propagandist.* Louisville: Photographic Archives, University of Louisville, 1977.

Anderson, Sherwood. *Home Town.* New York: Alliance Book Company, 1940.

Baldwin, Sidney. *Poverty and Politics: The Rise and Decline of the Farm Security Administration.* Chapel Hill: The University of North Carolina Press, 1968.

Bush, Martin H. *The Photographs of Gordon Parks.* Kansas: Edwin A. Ulrich Museum of Art, Witchita State University, 1983.

Capa, Cornell, ed. *The Concerned Photographer 2.* New York: Grossman Publishers, 1972.

Carlebach, Michael L. "Art and Propaganda: The FSA Photography Project." M.A. Thesis, Florida State University, 1980.

Carr, Carolyn Kinder. *Ohio: A Photographic Portrait 1935-1941.* Akron: Akron Art Institute, 1980.

Conkin, Paul K. *Tomorrow a New World: The New Deal Community Program.* Ithaca: Cornell University Press, 1959.

Dabney, Virginius. *Virginia: The New Dominion.* Charlottesville: The University Press of Virginia, 1971.

Delano, Jack. "Folklife and Photography: Bringing the FSA Home." *Southern Exposure* 5 (Summer/Fall 1979): pp.122-127.

Delano, Jack. Telephone Interview. March 15, 1985.

Dixon, Penelope. *Photographers of the Farm Security Administration: An Annotated Bibliography, 1930-1980.* New York: Garland Publishing, 1983.

Elliott, George P. *A Piece of Lettuce.* New York: Random House, 1957.

Evans, Walker. "Walker Evans, Visiting Artist." In *Photography: Essay and Images*, pp.315-317. Edited by Beaumont Newhall. New York: The Museum of Modern Art, 1980.

Garver, Thomas H., comp. *Just Before the War.* Balboa, California: Newport Harbor Art Museum, 1968.

Gutman, Judith Mara. *Lewis W. Hine and the American Social Conscience.* New York: Walker and Company, 1967.

Hardy, Forsyth, ed. *Grierson on Documentary.* New York: Praeger Publishers, 1966.

Heinemann, Ronald L. *Depression and the New Deal in Virginia: The Enduring Dominion.* Charlottesville: University Press of Virginia, 1983.

Hurley, F. Jack. *Portrait of a Decade: Roy Stryker and the Development of Documentary Photography in the Thirties.* Baton Rouge: Louisiana State University Press, 1972.

Hurley, F. Jack. *Russell Lee: Photographer.* Dobbs Ferry, New York: Morgan and Morgan, 1978.

Janis, Eugenia Parry, and MacNeil, Wendy, eds. *Photography Within the Humanities.* Danbury, New Hampshire: Addison House Publishers, 1977.

Katz, Leslie. "An Interview with Walker Evans." In *Photography in Print: Writings from 1816 to the Present*, p.363. Edited by Vicki Goldberg. New York: Simon and Schuster, 1981.

Kirsten, Lincoln. *Walker Evans: American Photographs.* New York: The Museum of Modern Art, 1938.

Lassiter, J. R. "Shenandoah National Park." *The Commonwealth*, July 1936, p.10.

Louisville, Kentucky. University of Louisville, Photographic Archives, Roy Stryker Papers.

Lynd, Robert, and Lynd, Helen. *Middletown: A Study in American Culture.* New York: Harcourt, Brace and Company, 1929.

MacLeish, Archibald. *Land of the Free.* New York: Harcourt, Brace and Company, 1938.

Maddox, Jerald C., ed. *Walker Evans, Photographs for the Farm Security Administration, 1935-1938*. New York: Da Capo Press, 1976.

Naef, Weston H., and Wood, James N. *Era of Exploration: The Rise of Landscape Photography in the American West, 1860-1885*. New York: Albright-Knox Art Gallery, The Metropolitan Museum of Art, 1975.

Newhall, Beaumont. "A Backward Glance at Documentary." In *Observations: Essays on Documentary Photography*, p.2. Edited by David Featherstone. Carmel, California: Friends of Photography, 1984.

Newhall, Beaumont. *Dorothea Lange Looks at the American Country Woman*. Fort Worth, Texas: Amon Carter Museum, 1967.

Newhall, Beaumont. *The History of Photography: From 1839 to the Present*. New York: The Museum of Modern Art, 1982.

Newman, Clarence W., ed. "Business Inventory." *The Commonwealth*, November 1940, p.3.

Newman, Clarence W. "Powder Output Begins at Radford." *The Commonwealth*, April 1941, p.7.

Nixon, Herman C. *Forty Acres and Steel Mules*. Chapel Hill: University of North Carolina Press, 1938.

Ohrn, Karin Becker. *Dorothea Lange and the Documentary Tradition*. Baton Rouge: Louisiana State University Press, 1980.

O'Neal, Hank. *A Vision Shared: A Classic Portrait of America and Its People, 1935-1943*. New York: St. Martin's Press, 1976.

Packett, John Rogers. *Five Photo-Textual Documentaries from the Great Depression*. Ann Arbor, Michigan: UMI Research Press, 1984.

Parks, Gordon. International Center of Photography, New York. Lecture, November 17, 1984.

Raper, Arthur, and Reid, Ira De A. *Sharecroppers All*. Chapel Hill: University of North Carolina Press, 1941.

Reeder, Carolyn, and Reeder, Jack. *Shenandoah Heritage: The Story of the People Before the Park*. Washington, D. C.: The Potomac Appalachian Trail Club, 1978.

Rifkind, Carole. *Main Street: The Face of Urban America*. New York: Harper and Row, Publishers, 1977.

Roosevelt, Franklin Delano. *Selected Speeches, Press Conferences, and Letters*. Edited by Basil Rauch. New York, 1957. Cited in William Stott, Documentary Expression and Thirties America, p.26. New York: Oxford University Press, 1973.

Rosenblum, Naomi. *A World History of Photography*. New York: Abbeville Press, 1984.

Rothstein, Arthur. *Arthur Rothstein: Words and Pictures*. New York: American Photographic Book Publishing Co., 1979.

Rothstein, Arthur. New Rochelle, New York. Interview, January 17, 1985.

Rouse, Parke, Jr. "Newport News and Defense." *Commonwealth*, June 1941, p.11.

Ryan, David D. "Sherwood Anderson's Hideaway in the Hills." *Commonwealth*, January 1981, p.37.

Sandburg, Carl. *Poems of the Midwest*. New York and Cleveland: World Publishing, 1946.

Scanlan, Glen. "Marketing Tobacco in Danville." *The Commonwealth*, November 1940, p.11.

Severin, Werner Joseph. "Photographic Documentation by the F.S.A., 1935-1942." M.A. Thesis, University of Missouri, 1959.

Shelton, Scott. "The Shenandoah National Park: Its Impact on a Mountain People." M.A. Thesis, Old Dominion University, 1962.

Siegel, Arthur. "Fifty Years of Documentary." In *Photographers on Photography*, p.90. Edited by Nathan Lyons. Englewood Cliffs, New Jersey: Prentice-Hall, 1966.

Smith, J. Russell. *North America*. New York: Harcourt, Brace and Company, 1925.

Steichen, Edward. *The Bitter Years: 1934-1941*. New York: The Museum of Modern Art, 1962.

Stryker, Roy E., and Johnstone, Paul H. "Documentary Photographs," in *The Cultural Approach to History*, p.328. Edited by Caroline F. Ware. New York: Columbia University Press, 1940.

U.S. Department of Agriculture, Farm Security Administration. *F.S.A. Annual Report, 1941*. Washington D.C.: Government Printing Office, 1942.

Vachon, Brian. "John Vachon: A Remembrance." *American Photographer*, October 1979, pp.34-45.

Vachon, John. "Tribute to a Man, an Era, an Art." *Harper's*, September 1973, pp.96-97.

Vance, Rupert B. *How the Other Half Is Housed: A Pictorial Record of Sub-minimum Farm Housing in the South.* Chapel Hill: University of North Carolina Press, 1936.

Washington, D.C. National Archives. Department of Agriculture, Farm Security Administration, Record Group 96.

Wertenbaker, Thomas J. *Norfolk: Historic Southern Port.* Durham, North Carolina: Duke University Press, 1962.

Williams, Richard L., ed. *Documentary Photography*, Life Library of Photography. New York: Time-Life Books, 1972.

Wilson, Charles Morrow. *Roots of America: A Travelogue of American Personalities.* New York: Funk & Wagnalls, 1936.

Wolcott, Marion Post. Letter. March 17, 1985.

Wolcott, Marion Post. Telephone Interview. March 14, 1985.

Wood, Nancy. *In This Proud Land: America 1935-1943, As Seen in the FSA Photographs.* New York: Galahad Books, 1973.

Wood, Roy. "Farm Tenancy in Virginia." M.A. Thesis, University of Virginia, 1948.

Wright, Richard, and Rosskam, Edwin. *Twelve Million Black Voices: A Folk History of the Negro in the United States.* New York: Viking Press, 1941.

Writers of the Works Project Administration. *The Negro in Virginia.* New York: Hastings House, 1940.

Writers of the Works Project Administration. *Virginia, A Guide to the Old Dominion.* New York: Oxford University Press, 1940.

Text type by Teagle and Little, Inc.,
ITC Garamond™ Book

Display type by B.F. Martin, Inc.,
ITC Garamond™ Ultra

Printed by Teagle and Little, Inc.,
on Warren Lustro Gloss cover and Warren Lustro Dull text

Black and white photographs reproduced as 150 line black and gray duotones
with spot varnish

Color photograph (cover) reproduced from a 4″ × 5″ transparency, lasar scanned
as a 150 line 4-color process

Designed and produced in Norfolk, Virginia